FREEDOM: A FIELD GUIDE

A NOT-SO-LINEAR JOURNEY TO YOUR OWN INNER COMPASS

LAURIE ANNE MCCAULEY

OnUpward

Publishing

PRAISE FOR LAURIE ANNE MCCAULEY

Reading Laurie's book felt less like consuming information and more like witnessing something being created—like a painting slowly emerging, brushed in rainbows under a quiet moon. There's a beautiful balance of clarity, compassion, and practicality throughout, inviting reflection without pressure. Rather than telling the reader what to think, it opens a space where insight can settle naturally and meaningful shifts can begin.

It's a gift from one vulnerable heart to another, if you're willing to receive her wisdom and share her desire for freedom of mind.

L. Fredrickson

"Laurie shakes us out of the branches of our own tree so we can see our life's hidden roots—adding humor, art, and poetry along the way. She shares her journey and distills life's essence into a grounded, clear, and deeply engaging read."

D. O'Foughlu, PhD, RPA

"A book like no other I have ever read. Every chapter is like a door opening to a new idea, thought, process, or memory. I can open the book anywhere and—POOF—I find myself immersed in a story that demands my attention, makes me smile, and makes me think. My favorite chapter? *Silence Please!*, because I really need to remember that! It's like taking a journey inside my head and heart to learn how to be free and content. This book will be my constant companion for many years."

P. Butler

"Punchy, definitely. Folksy casual. Approachable—not preachy or cerebral, not 'high falutin.' Easy to read. Very powerful, and this will help me next time I feel like yelling 'F-YOU' to my significant other!"

Anonymous

"I would recommend this book to anyone who isn't a skimmer in life —who is a bit freaked out or overwhelmed by existence, yet loves a good chat with people, especially strangers, to reinforce that there is goodness in the world and a reason for being. That we rub elbows at odd times with essential people we may never see again, but whose impact will last a lifetime. That our upbringing doesn't have to poison the rest of our lives. That we have always had what we are seeking.

This book brilliantly, humorously, and wisely navigates so many mind labyrinths we build for ourselves without even realizing it, and provides easy passage out. It's a delightful, inspiring visit—one that can be carried with you and enjoyed over and over."
- L. Miller

"Whether a seeker or a cynic, or somewhere in between, this book has insights that will resonate at some level for everyone. It contains wisdom born of experience—irreverent at times, funny often, never preachy—all wrapped up in a clear, approachable writing style."
L. Kalvaitis

DEDICATION

For my grandmother, Hazel Rose McCauley, who showed me that imagination is a strength, courage can be gentle, and love knows how to listen. She was my rock and never questioned what I saw, felt or sensed.

Gram, you saw me clearly from the very beginning—and that has made everything else possible. Thanks & Miss You!

PAUSE
TRUST
LET GO
LISTEN
faith
CARE
safe
secure
Shelter
Unconditional
Acceptance
Reliance
Rest
FREE
STOP
BREATHE
witness
wait
REST
OPEN
CALM
SURRENDER
YIELD
FOLD
RELENT
RELINQUISH
RELEASE
Kiss
Goodbye

It was mid-lockdown, May or June 2020. I'd already retired—twice. First, from a thirty-year corporate career helping women navigate school nutrition programs across all fifty states. Then from my own business, Onward & Upward, Inc., guiding seniors through the downsizing and moving maze. (Yes, I've got a thing for feeding and freeing people.)

My search for truth started decades earlier, back when I realized the Sunday School answers weren't cutting it anymore. Let's just say the whole heaven/hell binary started feeling off. So I did what any curious, twenty-something, slightly rebellious, spiritually hungry human might do: I wandered off-script and started poking around in the cosmic junk drawer to see what else might be out there.

I read the books. Took the workshops. Walked on coals. I've saged, journaled, artist-dated, chanted, and vision-boarded like my life depended on it. Crystals? Carried, cleansed, and full-moon charged. Sweat lodges, singing bowls, drumming circles, howling, humming—I did it all. karate, yoga, tai chi, and qigong. Walking meditations, running meditations, stairs-as-penance meditations. From beaches to mountains, from sea to shining sea—literally—I've practiced something in every one of the fifty states. The Native American Vision Quest in Moab, Utah was no spa weekend—ten days in the desert that left me so blissfully unscrambled I couldn't dial my own phone number at a rest stop on the way home. There was **David Elliott**'s transforming breath work, in LA, California, that made me see colors, **davidji** meditations where I totally left my body, and one silent retreat in Ireland where I spent the whole time sick in my room (my most successful silence to date).

Then came the great era of Releasing All The Things—fasting, acupuncture, colonics, acupressure, tapping, potions, tinctures, **The Emotion Code**, **Personal Power**, and hundreds of books, movies, and workshops in between—anything that claimed to free me from traumas or trapped emotions, real or imagined, past or present, this life or the last, physical or metaphysical. Allergies (**NAET - Nambudripad Allergy Elimination Technique**) viruses, maybe even a stray parasite—I cleared them all. Or at least tried to. Somewhere along the way, I became a Reiki Master and eventually a meditation teacher—not because I yearned to master the mysteries, but because I had to experience them thoroughly, deeply.

Then came the "anonymous" years—those circles of chairs that quietly taught me what surrender really means. That's where I learned how to move forward with honesty, openness, and willing-ness—not as lofty ideals, but as practical skills. Skills that later proved essential when meditation reappeared in my life, not as another thing to master or fix, but as the simplest, truest channel of all. Step Eleven, regardless of which **Twelve Step Program** you may follow, suggests prayer and meditation as daily maintenance. For me, prayer is still too broad—more trigger than tool—so I dropped the mic on meditation.

Show up. Sit down. Breathe. Repeat. No equipment required.

And then… something shifted. A tipping point, maybe. A world gone weird and unusually quiet. With fewer distractions and nowhere to run (literally), I stopped chasing tools and started listen-ing. Two minutes a day. Every day. No skipping, no optimizing, no spiritual theatrics. Just sitting. Just breathing. Long enough to hear what had been there all along.

And I stuck with it. Thirty days turned into sixty, then ninety, and counting. Not because I finally found the right method, but because I stopped trying to get somewhere else. I stayed put. I paid attention.

That's where this Field Guide begins. Not with answers, gurus, or guarantees—but with presence, curiosity, and a willingness to listen. What follows isn't a map with a destination. It's a collection of trail notes, missteps, markers, and reminders from someone who wandered widely, got a little lost on purpose, and eventually learned to trust the compass I'd been carrying the whole time.

———

———

This book is a field guide—not a how-to for dummies and not a memoir in the traditional sense. It isn't linear. Non-linear, by definition, simply means "not arranged or expressed in a straightforward, sequential way," which turns out to be a pretty good description of real life.

What you hold is a collection of real stories, lived insights, and moments when I got quiet enough to hear something true—for me. Sometimes it was a whisper. Sometimes a lightning bolt. Either way, it pointed inward.

Each essay/story stands on its own and is paired with an image and a poem. Together, they offer different ways in—sometimes through prose, sometimes through rhythm, sometimes through what catches your eye. The pieces are loosely grouped in a field guide format—because let's be honest: don't we all wish we had a dependable manual for this crazy life?

This is the guide I wish someone had handed me. Most of us aren't looking for more advice—we're looking for something that actually resonates. Something that helps us trust our own next step. Something that offers a quiet confirmation that you're not alone and instinctively heading in the best direction. That's what this guide is for. It won't give you the answers, but it might help you hear—and believe in—your own answers, if you're willing to pause and listen.

This book is intentionally non-linear. You can start anywhere, skip around, annotate, or even read it backwards. The goal isn't completion; it's connection. Listen for what clicks in you. Follow what draws you in. That's your DMGS speaking—your inner guidance system. I call it my Divine Magical Guidance System, an internal GPS you already have. This guide is simply an invitation to notice it, trust it, and follow where it leads.

Like any good field guide, this one reflects the terrain as it appeared at the time—weather subject to change. Some digital links are included as helpful waypoints and may evolve, move, or disappear over time; consider them optional invitations, not promises of eternal uptime. Sorry, not sorry.

You don't need to read this book in order. You don't need to agree with anything—or even finish it. Nothing here is meant to convince or convert you. What matters is noticing what draws you in, what makes you pause, what quietly says *this matters*. Take what resonates. Leave the rest. Let it flow or let it go!

Prose and story tend to engage the thinking mind. Poetry slips past it. Images do something else entirely. They orient you without words—offering a mood, a direction, a felt sense. You don't have to interpret any of it or get it "right." Look. Read. Skip. Linger. Let whatever wants to land, land. Worst case? You turn the page. Best case? Something awesome clicks before your brain has a chance to argue. This first poem opens the gate.

No Other Love

All there is to do – is listen
to your own heart
Follow your own song
to the beat of the drum within.
Do not despair or grow impatient
Like the tides ebb and flow –
as the seasons go
So turn the circles of your time.
Within each breath be grateful
Talk to me – Listen – Breathe
Gracefully your life unfolds
in time's time with wisdom and magic.
There is no other time but now.
There is no other love but ours.

Laurie Anne McCauley - January 2019

(This poem reflects the spirit of the entire book: a return to your own rhythm, your own knowing. It isn't a demand. It's a reminder. That listening is the way forward. That there's magic in the moment you pause long enough to hear past the static outside. Also, trail mix pairs well with epiphanies. Just saying.)

P.S. Some people think it's anathema to write in a book—especially a "nice" one. This isn't that kind of book. It's a field guide, meant for the trail: dirt, grime, rain, snow, maybe even ocean spray. There's nothing precious about it. Beat it up. Underline wildly. Fill the margins. I intentionally removed a lot of silly headers and footers so you'd have *space*—to scribble, argue, doodle, and make it yours. (Yes, that was a wink from your friendly neighborhood space creator.)

YOU'RE
INVITED

CONTENTS

PART FIVE
LANDMARKS & TRAIL MARKERS

PART SIX
WHAT I LEARNED OFF TRAIL

PART SEVEN
WHAT NOW? KEEP GOING!

TRAILHEAD
P i
NO FIRES

PART ONE
ESSENTIAL GEAR
SUPPLIED BY SOURCE
ALREADY INSTALLED

You're human—congrats. That comes with some wild, built-in gear: curiosity, resilience, intuition—and, drumroll, a biological miracle.

Whether you feel brilliant or broken—or a beautiful mess in between—you showed up fully loaded. Roughly 30–37 trillion cells working in concert. Eyes that catch nuance, ears that tune into tone, skin that feels truth in a breeze, taste buds that remember sweetness, and a nervous system that lights up before your mind catches on. And if one of those senses came online differently? The others recalibrate. This section is about the gear already in your backpack —often overlooked, rarely honored, but always available. Think of this as your base camp orientation. We'll dust off these powerful instruments, give them names—like your **Divine Magical Guidance System (DMGS)**—and learn to use them. No badge, manual, or guru required. And no, it's not sold separately.

OBSERVE
DON'T
JUDGE

ASK DON'T ANALYZE

BECAUSE THINKING
HARDER WASN'T WORKING

This little gem came to me a few days back: Ask, Don't Analyze. I've found that brief, succinct statements like this often hold the most power. Like a mantra, they interrupt my standard patterns of thought and behavior. Years ago, I created signs with phrases like "Notice, Don't Defend" and "Observe, Don't Judge." I hung them where I could see them often, printed and laminated copies to share, and repeated them aloud to myself—and to anyone within earshot. These simple messages carried so much peace and freedom once I started implementing them! I'm sure there are more, like "Laugh, Don't Compare," but that's a topic for another day.

Right now, Ask, Don't Analyze feels especially powerful because it speaks directly to my present awareness of a severe lack of trust. That's a harsh but honest way to put it. I'm building trust now—intentionally, patiently—through focus and practice. I'm learning to ask and listen to my own DMGS (Divine Magical Guidance System). I know I've mentioned this before, but maybe it's time to clarify.

I've always had a complicated relationship with the concept of God, shaped by my upbringing in a conservative Catholic household. I've come to see that it's not about God per se, but about people. It's a User Error—a human problem. I don't trust most humans. No hard feelings; I just sense that, understandably, most people are ultimately looking out for themselves. Without realizing it, I began relying on my DMGS when I started journaling in 1976, inspired by The Diary of Anne Frank. That connection has stayed with me ever since. Through my BYOB (Be Your Own Bestie - not Bring Your Own Beer!) meditation practice, I'm now learning how to listen more closely and hear more clearly. I'm discovering how to distinguish between illusion, delusion, and the quiet, steady voice of my DMGS.

This journey has also been shaped by practices like 2-Way prayer, publicized by The Oxford Group in the 1930s. It combines meditation and journaling—two of my favorite things! There's also a step where you check in with another person, but I've found that part less helpful. Even the most caring advice I've received has often been wrong or fear-based. Instead, I've turned to tools like muscle testing, as described by David Hawkins, to develop a more objective way of checking in. Slowly but surely, I'm learning to trust my DMGS and consult it often.

Ask, Don't Analyze. It's such a simple mantra, but it challenges me to step out of my old habits. Thoughts, I've learned, are often unhelpful distractions from the core of truth. Asking, on the other hand, is about opening up and receiving guidance. I also have to learn to sit with the answers I don't like—the ones that make me uncomfortable or push my boundaries. Discomfort tends to send me straight into avoidance, so I get to practice patience, trust, and moving forward anyway.

I'm amazed by how often the answer to my urgent, pressing question is simply, "It doesn't matter." Nothing puts me in my place quite like that! It's humbling, for sure, but also freeing. It reminds me that much of what I agonize over isn't as important as I think.

This is the beginning of my Ask, Don't Analyze mantra practice. I'm excited to see where it takes me. This simple phrase puts me in both the driver's seat and the passenger's seat of my life. It's a powerful reminder that I get to take full responsibility for my choices on every level—and that guidance is always there when I choose to ask for it.

Answers

What happens when it clicks
and the pieces fall in place?

What happens when you figure out
The only thing that stopped you
Was nothing more and nothing less
Than you?

And all your questions –
Answered –
Sit staring at your face?

And things you never figured
Would make any sense at all
Are there
beneath your fingertips
AND
You've got the ball!

- 2002

"This is a great truth, one of the greatest truths...Once we truly know that life is difficult - once we truly understand and accept it - then life is no longer difficult. Because once it is accepted, the fact that life is difficult no longer matters."
"Principle -- particularly moral principle -- can never be a weathervane, spinning around this way and that with the shifting winds of expediency. Moral principle is a compass forever fixed and forever true."
"A great deal of talent is lost to the world for want of a little courage. Every day sends to their graves obscure men whose timidity prevented them from making a first effort."
"Use the losses and failures of the past as a reason for action, not inaction."
"It is not so much what you believe in that matters, as the way in which you believe it and proceed to translate that belief into action."
"...you can choose to liberate the future."
"Reflect upon your present blessings, of which every man has many—not on your past misfortunes, of which all men have some."
LMC
10-24-24

SO.... THERE'S A GUARDIAN NOW?

CHERISHED ONE, THIS IS YOUR LIFE. RELEASE INTO IT.

That's me
the tiny bird
in the hole
in the dark
in the middle
of the mound
covered by words
and brambles
protected
thick and strong
hidden
pretending
I am safe
hidden
pretending
hidden,
I sense a radiance,
I shiver to touch it,
a brilliance like the sun
is that me too?

Next to me in this hole was a huge energy source. A power beyond limits. Right there on the ground beside me inside the mound piled high was authentic power, vibrant and pulsing with a frequency off the charts. Holy crap, it scares the hell out of me. All that power. What on earth would I ever do with that? I mean, am I supposed to just pick it up and go with it?

The energy source hummed like something alive, as if it held a language of its own, practically vibrating with potential I didn't yet trust myself to touch. It was beautiful and terrifying—a force both nurturing and consuming. What would I even become if I reached for it? And what if it decided it didn't want to stick around, leaving me with a one-way ticket to Imposter Syndrome Central?

During the BYOB (Be Your Own Bestie) **OSHO** meditation, they introduced the concept of a Guardian. It sounds kind of serious, but honestly, it's like having a bouncer for my soul—someone to keep an eye on the physical habits and behaviors that either keep me grounded or send me spiraling. The meditation invites you to ask this Guardian to toss out old patterns and bring in fresh new ones, as if we're in the life-habit equivalent of spring cleaning. But, of course, nothing's ever that easy. The Guardian might not reveal any grand wisdom right away because, apparently, decades-old behaviors don't just pack up and leave. Who knew, right?

As I sat in meditation, I could practically feel the Guardian giving me that look—the one that says, "You're finally ready, huh? Well, this is going to take some practice and courage." This figure, part gentle intermediary, part drill sergeant, part overprotective parent, was maintaining all the patterns I've perfected over the years. Comparing, judging, dodging responsibilities and hard conversations, doing mental gymnastics and numbing behaviors to avoid acknowledging my feelings—you name it, I had it down. I asked the Guardian to help me drop these like outdated fashion choices and maybe pick up something that actually fits who I am today.

Then I got this vision of a mound, a little like the one in my art piece, where the Guardian had wrapped me in this protective bubble. And sure, I was managing, feeling safe, maybe a little too cozy. But after this meditation, I know I'm ready for more. Here's the kicker, though: that insane power sitting next to me? I realized didn't even know that part of me existed. I sit in awe of the expansive freedom and joy available. The link between love, responsibility, and power is shown but not explained. I am still intent upon allowing Love to enter where there hasn't been any, possibly ever. I have no clue how this authentic power fits into the overall execution, practice, or picture I have for myself. I do get that consistency and stretch are required to continue the journey to expansion and serenity.

Patience and practice—two mantras that seem to love showing up on this path. I've realized that if the bird is ever going to fly, it's going to be one slow, cautious flap at a time. This power? I'm not here to bulldoze into it. I'll work with it every day, get to know it. Maybe with enough patience, I'll figure out what it's trying to teach me. But for now, I'm okay taking it one clumsy step at a time, letting the Guardian roll its eyes and sigh while I do my best not to get in my own way.

Vulnerable Joy

The lines are down,
fallen on the page.
The way I saw them
in my heart.
Everywhere I gaze
the outline of my life
is perfectly cast down.

Like pickup stix
that form a grand design,
hidden until now.

Like an obscure Rorschach blot
now reveals my imagined
image when the light,
is just so.

Not all-but many
of the pages of my
coloring book are drawn -
beautifully - gracefully
lovely - sketched.
Revealing my true hearts'
desire and passion.

"There it is - Cherished One.
Trust yourself.
This is your life,
release into it."

As I color the pages
adding more life
more depth
I pause - I wonder

I HAVE NO IDEA WHAT I'M DOING!
I'm vulnerable and grateful
for each perfect stroke!

-- January 2019

THE BRIDGE CALLED TRUST

STEPPING OUT OF SURVIVAL MODE

Every year, I choose a word—a compass for growth and intention. This year, my journey led me to Trust.

As I considered my five finalist words for 2025--Accept, Accountable, Commitment, Responsible, and Trust—it became clear that Trust was the foundation. Accept and Accountable felt too similar to Trust and Commitment, leaving me with a trio: Trust, Responsible, and Commitment. Without Trust, responsibility feels heavy, and commitment feels hollow. Trust had to come first.

And isn't that fitting? When I created the image above for this essay, I noticed that definitions from multiple sources included responsibility and commitment. Trust doesn't stand alone; it naturally gives rise to these other principles. Choosing Trust feels like choosing a trio, with Trust as the guiding star.

Trust what? Trust my DMGS (Divine Magical Guidance System)—that quiet, intuitive voice that guides me toward alignment. Trust my soul, my highest truth, my natural, relaxed knowingness. It's about trusting that even when I don't fully understand the "how," my inner guidance will lead me to what's right, in its own time. Trust is the foundation for listening, aligning, and acting with confidence, clarity and kindness.

While I was trolling about town a week or so ago, I wandered into a Barnes & Noble. I had done a quick Amazon search for a book that would assist with identifying trapped emotions. David Hawkins, in his book ***Letting Go: The Pathway of Surrender*** has a method for releasing emotions, and I wanted more options or ideas. (He uses muscle testing—there are plenty of videos on YouTube.) I was, as always, curious and open to additional techniques that could release this pent-up negative energy. I discovered a book called ***The Emotion Code*** by Dr. Bradley Nelson. Miracle of miracles, the physical bookstore had the book in stock, and I was able to satisfy my lust for information immediately. God wink? Synchronicity? Of course, why not! A foreword by Tony Robbins didn't hurt either!

The book builds on Hawkins' work, more details on muscle testing a chart of 60 emotions, yes/no flowcharts for subconscious communication, and actionable techniques to release the pent up emotions. It's designed to help identify whatever emotions are ready to be released and send them packing. (Where do they go, I wonder?) I devoured the book in an afternoon and immediately began reviewing the website I could see that there are classes and certifications and I decided to search for certified practitioners online. This way I could ask questions directly and get a better feel for how the techniques worked in real life.

My first session was with a novice practitioner, and while her energy and enthusiasm were wonderful, the timing wasn't ideal. Tango, our beloved patriarch guinea pig, passed away in my arms shortly afterward, and I was too immersed in real-time grief to fully process the release. It was a deeply emotional moment—such a beautiful, innocent little life. OUCH!

Several days later, once my emotions had settled, I reached out to a different practitioner from the Emotion Code website. This woman had years of experience, and it showed in her confidence, speed, and methodical approach. The session felt transformative. She guided me through releasing multiple trapped emotions from early in my life—emotions I always knew were there but had no idea how to let go of. The practitioner I found, ***Juanita Ecker***, thank you!

I left feeling lighter and freer, and she even assigned me homework to help me practice identifying and releasing emotions on my own. This work, grounded in trust, felt like a massive success. I'm looking forward to continuing sessions and deepening my ability to clear out the "clouds" that block the light of Spirit.

With Trust, I am able to move forward intuitively to remove

those clouds. Trust allows me to release old emotions, align with my DMGS, and act from a place of confidence and love. This year, I'm stepping out of survival mode. I'm choosing to thrive—in awareness, in alignment, and in the freedom to fully participate in life.

Guide

Hours fly unhindered.
Days pass, stampeding.
Today soon yesterday.
Tomorrow gone forever.

Pray that each fleeting hour,
Each hastening day,
Brings joy or peace
To some heart.

Use talent,
Cultivate skill.
Waste not your unique gifts
In idle selfish play.

There is purpose in pain.
Life in death.
And joy in giving your life
To love
every soul.

No discrimination,
No judgment,
No deception.
You are no worse,
Nor any better than any soul,
Only different.

Help and love,

And need your neighbor.
Don't teach, only learn.
And thru learning,
You may guide.

- 1989

DMGS

PERHAPS IT'S TIME

TUNE IN AND TRUST THE DMGS!

The holidays have come and gone so quickly. This year felt different —odd, even. We didn't decorate or get particularly nostalgic or sentimental. I found myself immersed in something far more transformative: my afternoon BYOB (Be Your Own Bestie) meditations. I'm noticing a distinct difference in how I experience everyday routine tasks and engage with people. This year, my new perspective seemed to wrap itself around the season, making even the simplest moments feel transformed—like my meditations or the quiet realization of what I'd been missing.

It's a paradox, isn't it? Since I've gone totally selfish in my pursuits and goals, my experience is actually less selfish and self serving. Now that I recognize when I'm being SELF-manipulative, controlling, worried about being right, defending, looking good, or fixing everything—and practice letting go of all that—I see my environment and the people in it so differently. I see them with love and compassion. Now that kindness and compassion are becoming more normal inside of me, they're leaking to the outside. Did someone tell me this might happen? Ha, turns out they were right!

Seeing family this year, it struck me, for the first time in 17 years, how much I've been blocking intimacy and missing the chance to create real connections. Without the usual pity party or the expectation that someone should hang on my every word of wisdom, I see it so clearly: I am not a victim at all. Good grief, Laurie Anne! I am responsible. And I can proceed with clear, kind, and loving intentions. When I saw my niece smile as we talked, I realized how much I'd been missing these simple moments of connection. The warmth I felt wasn't from their validation—it was from finally being present. No need to beat myself up for what's past. There's also nothing urgent to fix—just options, a sense of space, and openness for what I may choose to create in the future.

Holy shit... the gifts just keep revealing themselves.

Yesterday, I went shopping for our New Year's Eve dinner. (We also met on New Year's Eve 2007, so it's our 18th anniversary.) Typically, we enjoy crab legs, white rice, freshly cooked artichokes with loads of butter, and something sweet and decadent to finish. This year, we decided on lobster instead of crab for a change. My shopping trip was outstanding. These days, I bundle errands to limit trips to town, going once every couple of weeks. It makes each trip feel like a treat, an adventure—a fabulous opportunity to move slowly and take in every magical moment. During this trip, I finally used my training to pause and intentionally check in with inner wisdom about certain purchases—food, supplements, etc. I was surprised to notice how aware I felt. Often, I was singing quietly or just giddy with joy. Such a fucking awesome way to move through the world! I'm so grateful and finally actually tuned into my very own DMGS—Divine, Magical, Guiding System. It's more than just a concept—it's become a constant guide, a way to move through life with intention, ease, and a sense of wonder.

It took me a while this morning to land on that particular acronym, but it perfectly expresses my experience. It's also internal, intuitive, and so many other things. "Divine"—for sure. "Magical"—no doubt. Sweetly "Guiding"—absolutely. "System" nods to the fact that it's always been there, part of my DNA, waiting for me to notice. Whether I was resistant, distracted, or just forgot doesn't matter now. I've got the number, the position on the radio dial to tune in anytime, every time. Once again, I am exceedingly grateful, overwhelmingly relieved, and blissed out! Happy Holidays to me!

As the year draws to a close, I'm reveling in the simplest magic —awareness, gratitude, and the sheer joy of being. This holiday season didn't need decorations or fanfare. The gifts were already here, hidden in plain sight, waiting for me to notice. Happy Holidays, indeed.

Perhaps It's Time?
I grow weary
of the doubting
and self-loathing.
I am tired of
feeling alone
and unloved.
Perhaps it's time
to shed these
beliefs? These
habitual - cultural
illusions and delusions?

Perhaps it is time
to just set them
off - to the side
and explore what
IS - REAL - REALITY?

I grow weary of
the battle ground
I've become.
I am tired of the defending
fighting & resistance.
Perhaps it is time
for surrender
to lay down
my fears
and expectations?
my judgements
and attachments?

Perhaps it is time
for love?
Perhaps it is safe
at last?
Perhaps I am enough,
brave enough,
strong enough
to let go
for real(ity) at last...

- April 10, 2022

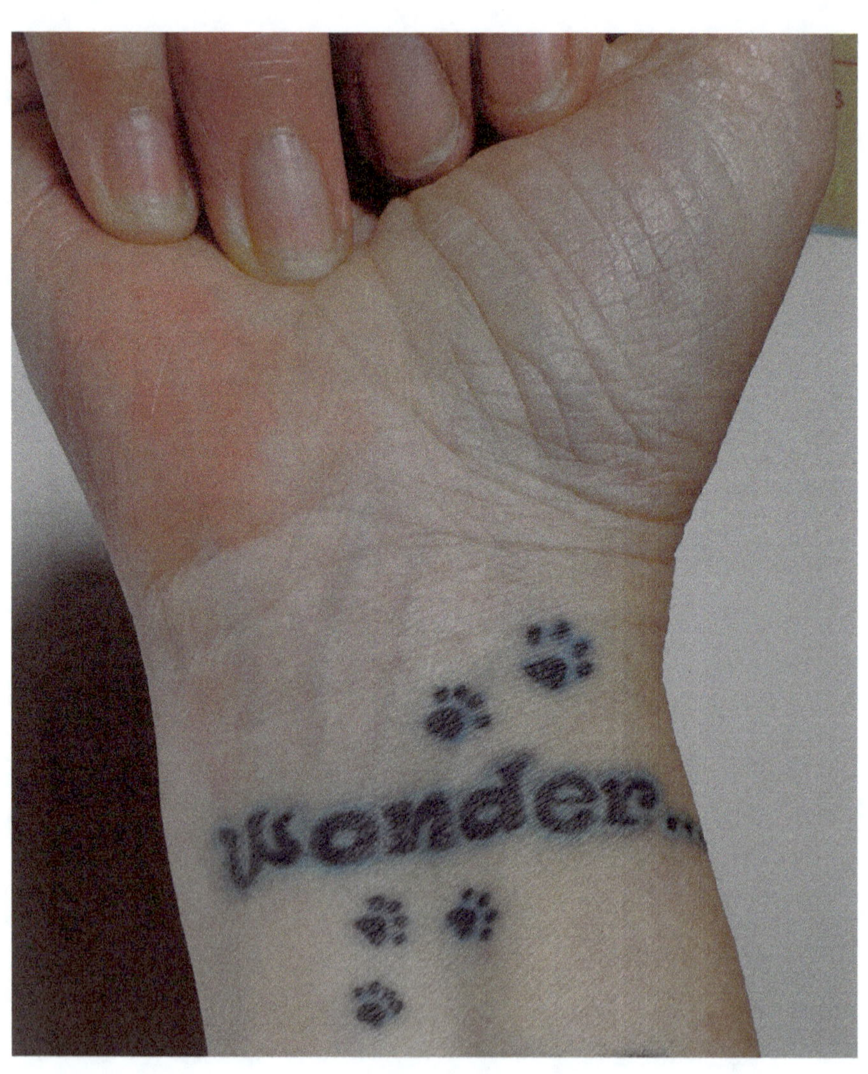
wonder...

PAWS TO WONDER

IT'S NOT A TIGER -
IT'S JUST A TRIGGER

I was chatting with my friend Sally, who had just landed what could be her dream job. She's trying to stay open-minded, bless her, but so far it's been more nightmare than dream. The onboarding is chaotic —scattered training, unclear expectations, too many projects, not enough time or money. Add in a clientele that behaves more like middle schoolers in detention than adults—gossip, drama, ego explosions   and it's no wonder she's feeling frayed.

Her first instinct? Run. Her second? Cry. I could feel both in my own body as she spoke. I managed to sneak in a whisper: "Remember, you can't control anyone's behavior. But you do get to choose how you respond." In that moment, I remembered something I've leaned on a lot: the way other people act is totally outside my control. REALLY! Let that sink in and notice how even when you think you know this, you keep trying to fix and control people or harbor unrealistic and un-communicated expectations for which you totally hold them accountable.   That's been one of the most surprising discoveries of the last few years: even in chaos, there are still choices OTHER than expecting, controlling, fixing and blaming. Not comfortable, not easy ones, and not always obvious, but they're there—often hidden inside the pause. It's easy to forget that in the gut punch of a powerful trigger. Step one: ride the trigger's adrenaline surge without biting anyone's head off. Step two: do your best poker face and maybe keep your mouth shut for a beat. Or five.

Every new job—every new anything, really—comes with a grab bag of grace and grit. There are boundaries to test and people to decipher. Friend or foe? Fickle or solid? Kind or kind of terrifying? The hard part is remembering that it's not your job to fix anyone or earn your worth by changing them. If someone's behavior lights up your nervous system like a pinball machine, great! You just found a button you'd lost track of. Time to uninstall.

Yippee, another chance to practice OHR (Observe Honor Release) - Observe the reaction (especially the physical bits; the heat, the heart racing, the flushed face), Honor the emotion, then Release - let it go. Not because it's "spiritually correct," but because it's *liberating*. Then, I get to ask the fun question: what else is possible here? More interesting choices, guaranteed. Especially if I remember: You are safe. You are not in danger. All is well, even if it's loud, clunky, or weird.

Still, it's wild how often I forget that. Especially in the moment. My first reaction, more often than I'd like to admit, is still to blame, defend, escape, or shut down. Sometimes I argue—in my head, out loud, with the person or with a completely imaginary version of them. Occasionally all at once. But every now and then, I catch it before it spills out. A half-second of space. Just enough to breathe. Why is it so hard to see our choices in the moment? Because our first instinct isn't usually wisdom. Mine sure isn't. It's some cocktail of defensiveness, blame, argument, or avoidance. Flight or fight or... snarky internal monologue. But if I can hold my tongue long enough not to lash out or run away, that's already a win.

I have a tattoo on my right wrist to help me remember. It says *WONDER*—woven with tiny animal paw prints running through it. The message? *Paws to Wonder.* Pause to wonder. And yes, that pun was absolutely worth etching into my skin. Because there's no access to choice without the pause. If I'm barreling down the trail of panic or projection, the path narrows to one: react. But if I pause? Oh, the wild freedom that lives in that moment.

The truth is, the "essential gear": I have a choice in every situation. Always. I can curse or bless. Sit still or phone a friend. Storm out or stay silent. There are always at least five options, even if one of them is "wait and see." And as fun as it might feel to act like a toddler ("I don't wanna and YOU can't make me!") or a teenager ("You're wrong and I'm leaving!"), those knee-jerk reactions don't get me where I actually want to go.

These days, I experiment with pretending I'm an actual grown-up. It's strangely effective. Especially when paired with another discovery: I'm allowed to take my time. No rush! Even when everything in me screams for quick resolution or escape, I've learned—often the hard way—that time and space are choice's best friends. Being present _to_ a choice and having the ability _to choose_ are not the same thing. I may have every tool in the toolbox, but if I'm too spun out to reach for them, they don't help much. The pause is the reach.

I'm not talking about life-or-death situations here. Our brilliant nervous systems will always kick in if a tiger shows up. But let's be honest: for most of us, "life-threatening" is almost never the case. Ego-threatening? All the time. Which is why we need to train ourselves to pause—to notice the difference. You're not being hunted. You're just being triggered. These days, I'm trying to notice that too—just notice it—without making it wrong. It's just one more data point in this strange and beautiful dashboard called being human.

When I think about Sally and her new job, I can feel that edge—the tipping point between curiosity and collapse. I've walked it so many times. The story she chooses to tell about what's happening makes a huge difference in how she may move through it. Her DMGS may start asking different questions: What if this is the dream job, just not the dream I expected? What would it feel like to let it unfold slowly, without demanding instant clarity?

OMG, this is the "adult" thing to do, right?! I get to ask myself: "So what do I _want_ this experience to feel like? How do I want to walk through this opportunity, this challenge, this invitation to grow? Journaling helps. So does meditation. And, yes, so does tattooing reminders on my wrist if that's what it takes to remember: I can pause. I can wonder. I can choose. I recently faced a personally tough decision, and a **_John Kabat-Zinn_**-inspired decision-making meditation showed up right on cue. I listened. I paused. And the answer arrived with far less drama than expected. Yeah—thank you.

The pause isn't passive. It's a portal to power and the most underrated tool in my essential gear. The one that turns chaos into curiosity, and reactivity into reflection. Even if nothing around me changes, something inside always does. And from there, I see more: five quiet doors creaking open, each one a possibility I couldn't access while pounding on the old, familiar one. So when I forget (because I will), I've got this tattoo, this practice, this reminder: Paws to wonder. It changes everything.

Breathe

Yet another man
Throws my life
Spinning
Into a whirlpool
I plunge, out of breath
I breathe water
Like air
I twirl and dance
The swirling water
Pulling me downward
The light from above
Dimmer
A feeling of dis-ease
Comes and I break
From the gravity of it all
I remember
I breathe air – not water
Shooting to the surface
Continuing my journey
The air and the sun
The river, my friends
Rapids ahead – ho –
It's good to feel!

- 2001

FOXHOLE NOT FORTRESS

A TENDER MAP BACK TO MYSELF

"I have been a seeker and I still am, but I stopped asking the books and the stars. I started listening to the teachings of my soul." – Rumi

For most of my life, I've been the classic overpacked wanderer. A seeker dragging a bulging backpack full of tools, tips, truths, and tangled directions. I chased constellations and cracked open retreat workbooks like they held the way to the Holy Grail. If a practice promised results, I tried it. But somewhere along the trail, I internalized the wisdom of **Rumi** and began tuning "in" instead. Not to the gurus, the stars or the books—but to something quieter. Something native. Something already inside.

It was during a recent morning meditation themed around trust and love that something deep began to shift. Not a big bang or a sudden insight—just a steady, soft unraveling. I've had emotional releases before while sitting in stillness, but this was different. Not dramatic or chaotic—just exquisitely tender. Quiet sobbing. Tears whispering trails on my cheeks, heart pulled wide open. No story, no reason. Just waves. I didn't try to analyze it or chase the "why." For once, I simply let it come. Let it wash me. Blow my nose. Move on. Except this time, I didn't move on. Not right away. I lingered with the afterglow, the imagery, the warmth. The emotional weight had opened something I didn't want to close back up.

What I wanted wasn't to understand it with my mind but to honor it with presence. I picked up a pen. What emerged wasn't a journal entry or an explanation. It was a poem. And shortly after, a conversation—more like a dictation. From a voice I've come to call *Ev (rhymes with "rev")*. Short for *Evollla*, my mashed-up, reversed spelling of "All Love." Another name for my DMGS (Divine Magical Guidance System) the quiet voice of inner truth I've started to trust more than all the external shouting.

The essence of that experience was unmistakably affectionate. The imagery was physical—hugs, cuddles, warmth. I wasn't alone in this vision; I was held. Cradled. Cherished. The weeping wasn't grief exactly. It was the ache of remembering something so real it makes this world feel a little less so. I noticed how incredibly vulnerable I felt in that state—so raw, so open, and also so beautiful. No armor. No performing. Just tenderness. And then something even deeper surfaced: homesickness. A bone-deep longing, not for a person or place on Earth, but for some realm just behind the veil— something I've always known but can't quite name.

I didn't resist it. I didn't try to fix it. I let the energy move through me like wind. The emotion didn't need an explanation. It just needed space. And in that space, I realized something subtle and enormous: I can go back. Not just during meditation, but anytime. This inner refuge—what I now call my foxhole—isn't a metaphorical escape hatch. It's essential gear. A kind of built-in shelter I forgot I had—camouflaged in the thicket of daily noise, but always there when I pause long enough to look. It's mine. Always accessible, always welcoming. I don't need a key or a code. Just willingness.

That's the practice now. To return. To visit the foxhole not just when I'm raw or unraveling, but whenever I want to reconnect with that part of me that already knows. That remembers. That loves. I wrote the poem below not as a conclusion but as a compass—a map back to that moment, that place.

My Foxhole
My inner sanctum
has hugs.
deep and warm
cushy and soft.
Safe, loving embraces.

My foxhole
has freedom
security
tears of joy

and cozy snugness.

Words fall short
expressing the
cherishment I feel
in there.

There is nothing
missing except
Judgement – Fixing
Fear and Worry.
(Past - Present - Future)

Going in I get to notice
these and leave them
in the umbrella stand or
on the mudroom hooks.

"Aww – There YOU are!"
a kindly voice
vibrates (it's Ev!).

In my innocent
vulnerable sweetness.
I am all beauty and fragrance,
no thorns or flaws.

I am held, leaning back
gently sobbing
tears flow warm
tickling my cheeks.

Beloved I am.
Treasured,
caressed – stroked
with gentle kindness.

Soothing coos
Immortal grace
brilliant arms
fold solid, firm.

Delicate attention
Listening – knowing
My deepest soul weeps.
No words.

Wave upon wave
I am loved,
treasured, cherished
accepted, understood.

Unconditional
tenderness lives
breathes – waits
in the shelter of
my foxhole.

My refuge echoes
reflections
and shadows
of my home.

My true home
is not here
Not in this plane,
time or form.
And I am very, very
homesick.

- June 2025

So I've added this to my inner field kit—not as a shiny new tool
I've mastered, but as a well-worn map to a place I now know exists.

A secret passage to an inner safe house. My foxhole isn't just a last resort anymore, or some mysterious floodgate that opens during meditation. It's a real-time option. A practice in progress. My intention—_loose but loving_—is to visit more often. To duck in moment by moment as I travel this trail and stumble across rough terrain, tangled emotions, or, you know… mean, shitty people. (Or perfectly lovely people having spectacularly shitty days.) Remember I am safe and loving. With a little repetition and a lot of curiosity, maybe this sacred shelter will stop feeling like an escape—and start feeling like home base. So, stay tuned - I'm learning to use this essential gear without accidentally crushing the daylights out of it.

JUST
shut up and
Listen

SILENCE PLEASE!

TURNS OUT MY BODY
HAD SOMETHING TO SAY

On October 23, 2024, I joined an OSHO International course with the impressively long title ***Reminding Yourself of the Forgotten Language of Talking to Your BodyMind***. Naturally, I shortened it to the BYOB meditation—*Be Your Own Bestie* (not Bring Your Own Beverage).

The course, which runs through November, includes optional facilitator training—something that immediately triggered my familiar urge to give it all away. *How could I teach this? Share it? Facilitate it?* I notice this thought pattern a lot when I sit. These days, I'm practicing pausing long enough to actually receive the experience myself before racing ahead. Anyway… I digress.

The course is structured, entirely online through Zoom, and involves minimal verbal interaction. There's a warm welcome and clear guidance, but unlike the more interactive No Mind class, this one encourages a quiet, inward focus. A "mild" trance state is recommended, with no need for conscious thought, analysis, or note-taking—just a connection with the inner realms. The feeling is mysteriously serene, urging stillness and a reawakening to this "forgotten language." My main takeaway from the first session was unmistakably clear: "LISTEN." When I later created art, I added the wry reminder, "JUST shut up and LISTEN."

What does it mean to truly listen? For me, it requires suspending distracting, often unhelpful thoughts—judgment, expectations, and especially the reflex to analyze or defend my perspective. True listening invites honesty, openness, and a willingness to stay present despite these distractions. It's challenging, as both internal voices and physical, environmental aspects conspire to derail the focus. Still, each return to the subject of the listening deepens the practice, making this practice a transformative process.

The command to "listen" may seem simple but not easy. Yet it's anything but simple. It encapsulates complex layers of spiritual, mental, and physical insight, shaping an intention that could serve as a core principle throughout life. Much like Love, Power, or Responsibility, it's fundamental to the balance of genuine compassion and self-expression. Do you hear the creative muse? The guiding parent? The subtle messages from your own body?

Our facilitator reads from a script during the 50-minute sessions, rich in language that prompts breakthrough perspectives. Each body part seems to have its own way of communicating—through images, feelings, memories, and even words. To interpret these subtle cues requires discernment and a gentle patience. I get the impression that the body is shy, like a meek animal hidden in the woods. You must sit in the clearing for hours just to catch a glimpse. I hope this is not the case. I have patience, but not that much patience.

As I settle into each session, I feel the boundaries of my awareness shifting, growing more sensitive to the body's signals. It's like tuning into a low-frequency radio station that becomes clearer as I let go of distractions. I am, for the first time, learning to "hear" my body speak in a language uniquely its own. What it offers in terms of insight is astounding and humbling.

Reflecting on the course so far, I feel this practice could go well beyond the meditation sessions. This understanding of deep listening could influence my life in subtle but powerful ways. I find myself more attuned to my body in daily moments, like a quiet undercurrent of awareness. This awareness touches my relationships, too, encouraging me to listen without immediately thinking of my response or opinion.

Already, I'm sensing shifts in how I approach daily interactions. By simply listening—without jumping to conclusions, judgments, or responses—I find a new ease in connecting with others. Conversations feel less pressured, more fluid, as I allow my own silence to create space for what truly needs to be expressed. This shift in focus is affecting how I handle challenges as well; by first tuning into the body's response to a stressful moment or difficult news, I feel more grounded and centered, better equipped to respond rather than react.

I also sense this approach deepening my creativity. There's a curious interplay between listening and creating: by silencing the mind, I'm better able to hear intuitive nudges and ideas that seem to emerge from within. Rather than "trying" to create, I feel as though I'm receiving insights from a quieter, more authentic place. This practice is beginning to feel like an essential ingredient in accessing a deeper layer of creativity, one that feels effortless and profoundly connected.

I'm eager to continue this journey, to discover the language of my own body, and perhaps even cultivate a new way of being—a kind of openness that transcends traditional listening. This is listening as an act of reverence, a way to honor my body, emotions, and inner self. The urge to "teach" or facilitate remains, but it now feels less like an obligation and more like an inevitable outcome of living this new awareness. I can't yet say what the full impact of this practice will be, but I'm excited to find out.

Stay tuned—I'm listening.

The Corner Café
I'm drawn to
Quiet, local places
Where frequency
Breeds familiar kindness.
And even the
Most brisk waiter
Is won over in time.
Where old men gather
And young lovers meet
Where the sea is near
And the sunset
An event.

I love to watch
And listen
And come again
At the same time
Or a different time
To stay awhile

And watch the shifts change.
To identify the owner
And the gossip
And the flirt.
To watch the response
Of each to strangers
And friends.

- 2001
Paris, France

PART TWO
GETTING YOUR BEARINGS
WHEN SOMETHING LANDS - KEEP IT CLOSE, LET IT SETTLE

Baseline truths: Gravity is real, quicksand exists, and you're not the center of the Universe…?

Welcome to Earth, babe. Population: complex. Rules: invisible, often unknowable, and utterly non-negotiable. You arrived with a miraculous sensing body. Now it's time to get your bearings. Thriving on this spinning rock requires a mix of rule-bending and realignment. Time stretches and contracts. Change never asks permission. Flow is real, but so is friction. And just when you think you've got the route all figured out, the trail disappears.

This section is about orientation—not to your ideal life, but to reality itself. To the wild tension of living in a world that's both unpredictable *and* governed by laws. These essays explore how to play with that paradox—how to let gravity ground you without holding you down, how to meet change without losing your center, how to stop trying to control the unchangeable and use it instead as a spiritual launching pad.

You won't find certainty here, but you might just find clarity. You don't need a map—just the humility to stop resisting and the guts to shimmy with paradox.

Untied
UNTETHERED...
RELEASED
LET GO
FLY
SET FREE
DETACHED

POWERFUL QUESTIONS, QUIET ANSWERS

FOR THOSE WILLING TO PAUSE AND LISTEN.

Lately, I've been fascinated by the power of questions. How do we ask the right ones? How do we recognize the answers? These are central to my understanding of DMGS (Divine Magical Guidance System), and as I dig deeper into different perspectives, I find new language to refine my own knowing. That's why Gary Zukav's discussion on intuition and awareness in *The Seat of the Soul,* struck me so deeply.

"To the five-sensory personality (5P), intuitive insights or hunches occur unpredictably and cannot be counted upon. To the multisensory personality (MP), intuitive insights are registrations within its consciousness of a loving guidance that is continually assisting and supporting its growth. Therefore, the multisensory personality strives to increase its awareness of this guidance." (Page 65)

To Zukav, the difference between a five-sensory and a multisensory personality is profound: one dismisses intuition as an oddity, the other sees it as a direct line to something greater. I love this distinction because it perfectly captures what I've been experiencing myself. The more I trust my DMGS, the clearer the promptings become.

Zukav expands on this idea by explaining that insights, intuitions, hunches, and inspirations are not random occurrences but messages from the soul—or from advanced intelligences assisting the soul on its evolutionary journey. The multi-sensory person, he says, honors intuition in a way the five-sensory person does not. To the five-sensory individual, these moments of knowing are mere curiosities. To the multi-sensory individual, they are prompts and links to a higher intelligence—one of greater comprehension and compassion.

> *"The first step to this awareness is becoming aware of what you are feeling. Following your feelings will lead you to their source. Only through emotions can you encounter the force field of your own soul."*

He provides an example of a husband's reaction to his wife working late. Instead of blindly reacting, he suggests asking powerful questions: Why does the news of this meeting affect me this way? Why do I still feel disturbed? Perhaps I don't trust that she would really prefer to be with me? Does my experience support my suspicion? What is my motivation?

Zukav emphasizes that we may not always be capable of hearing the answers when we ask, and the answers may not always come in ways we expect. Sometimes they come in the form of a feeling—a yes-feeling or a no-feeling. Other times, they arrive as a memory, a sudden thought that seems random at first, or even a dream. Sometimes the answer unfolds through an experience that occurs the next day. But, as he reminds us, *"Ask and you shall receive"* is *the rule, but you must learn how to ask and how to receive."*

Each time I read something like this and connect the dots to my own experiences, I'm flabbergasted! Just yesterday, I was talking with Juanita about the power of questions. Before that, I was discussing the Socratic method with someone else. And now, here is Zukav, insisting that questions—when asked with sincerity—always receive an answer.

But what really stands out to me is his emphasis on *feelings* as the pathway. Without the *pause*—that essential gap between stimulus and response—it's nearly impossible to recognize these intuitive answers. Without that stillness, we get swept up in conditioned reactions, triggering someone else's reaction, setting off an unconscious domino effect. The pause isn't just helpful—it's essential for untangling what's actually happening inside.

I reorganized some of Zukav's words for clarity, but his message is crystal clear. The answers we seek are already available within us. We've just never been taught precisely how to ask the right questions or how to listen for the answers. This pretty clearly defines my current mission! My practice of tuning into feelings aligns exactly with what he describes, but what I hadn't articulated fully until now is how essential it is to develop the ability to *receive* the answers as well.

So now, I ask: what questions am I ready to hear the answers to? And what about you?

To My Other

Why, my love
Am I so easily distracted?
from myself?
from you?
borne away, pulled, tugged
spirited and seduced?

While all I need
is you
is here
is now
my kismet
While all I truly want
is before and inside
my own mystery…

Even when I'm in solitude
the judgement and meanness
conspires and lurks
in my thinking.
My own thoughts
machinate distractions…

Why is that love?

Love's answer:
So you can remember, of course.
Explore and create

Overcome and blunder
Flounder and persist
This is only Earth, love,
the land of paradox and relativity.
It is not who you are.
It is only where you are now,
to experience and create and play
with who you are
with who we are
with Essence with Amity
with Precious
Have no fear.

- April 2020

When in
doubt
PAUSE

When angry
PAUSE

When hungry
PAUSE

And when you
pause...
BE STILL
and
KNOW

THE PAUSE IS THE PORTAL

THE ART OF LETTING CLARITY FIND YOU

The practice of pausing is paying off. I actually find myself, in a moment of decision, stopping—checking in with my inner teacher, DMGS (Divine Magical Guidance System), whatever-you-want-to-call-it. And frequently, the answer that comes back is the same: *"It doesn't matter."* At first, this response felt dismissive—like some cosmic brush-off. But the more I listen, the more I realize: the pause itself is the answer. In that space, the pressure to "get it right" disappears. The illusion that every choice is critical, every moment leading to some fateful, inescapable outcome, starts to dissolve. I had this unreasonable expectation that with synchronicity and *"God winks"* everywhere, every decision I made had to be deeply significant, leading me down a perfect magical path to a perfect outcome. Yikes, that's pressure.

But again: *"It doesn't matter."* This phrase shows up in the simplest places. Should I call so-and-so? Should I go to this meeting or that one? Should I email or write or meditate now? Should I buy this or that? Should I say something or stay still? Turns out, most of the time, it really doesn't matter. The level of gravity I place on these questions is often just a reflection of my own anxiety, my need to control things, my craving for certainty. But pausing pulls me out of that spiral. Instead of gripping onto the decision, I get to step back and witness—without urgency, without attachment, without weight.

The pause is everything. It is the space between impulse and action, where I get to question my automatic reactions instead of being dragged along by them. When I hit the pause button, I interrupt the script. I make room for something new. It's in that moment that I get to ask: *Is this real? Is this necessary? Is this true?* Without the pause, I react from habit. From old conditioning, old fears, old expectations—many of which aren't even mine. Cultural beliefs. Family narratives. The shoulds, the musts, the knee-jerk justifications and rationalizations that keep me locked in patterns I don't even realize I'm repeating. Pausing is the antidote. It's the simplest, most radical way to reclaim awareness, choice, and honesty in real time.

Who, me? Pretentious? Grandiose? Just a tiny bit pompous? What? No! SLAP! Amazing how simple and unemotional the response in my mind appears, smooth and quiet, like water over stone: *"It doesn't matter. And... it's OK."* But occasionally, if I sit with the silence just a moment longer, I'll hear something else: *"But... it would be fun to ______."* Sometimes the nudge makes sense. Other times, it's totally unexpected. And in that moment, fun replaces force, ease replaces overthinking, and I just... follow it.

Then, there are the times when the pause doesn't bring peace—it brings something darker. Lately, I've been present to a lack of self-confidence, a smoke-like saboteur lingering at the edges of my awareness. The voice of self-doubt, rebellion, resistance. I recognized it instantly—the same one I fought during my Never Binge Again era. The part of me that hates being contained.

Pause. *"It doesn't matter."* But then another whisper: *"You may want to allow it. Explore it."* Really? That seems scary and odd. Shouldn't I try to whisk it away with some happy color or ignore it until it leaves on its own? Oh. Here's a chance to actually practice what I've learned. Allow it. Explore it. Observe, honor, release. And when I do—when I sit with it instead of fighting it—I see it clearly: the hatred is just fear. The fear is grounded in not feeling safe.

So I try something different. As an experiment, I spent an entire day repeating a simple phrase: *"I am safe."* Every spare open space in my thoughts, I filled with it. I paused to remind myself: I am safe. That is all. No long explanation. No overanalyzing. And then I asked: *Does that apply right now?* To this English muffin? To this car ride? To this song on the radio? To this conversation, this feeling, this thought? And you know what? It did.

Pausing gave me the space to notice reality instead of assumption. To separate feeling unsafe from actually being unsafe. To recognize how often my thoughts create tension where there is none. *The pause is truth serum.* It asks: *What's actually happening, right now?* Not the story, not the fear, not the future projection. Just now. So, I keep pausing. I keep asking, *"Does this actually matter?"* and listening for the answer. And more often than not, I hear the same thing: "Nope. Not today it doesn't."

But what does matter? Presence. Curiosity. The ease that comes when I stop chasing and start trusting. The choice to rewrite the patterns that no longer serve me. The ability to step outside my habitual responses and meet life as it is—not as I assume it to be. That's what the pause reveals every time. And shit, that matters.

Choices

Choices to be made
Dice to be tossed
Do I trust the outcome?
Yes!
I trust in the dice
Every time
The dice I know

So when we
Decide – against principals
But without choice
And recognizing a lesson
Is that ok?

Look at what I
Was convinced to do
Lay off four people
The numbers convinced me
Numbers are power
Statistics rule

The time of the bear
The West…
What a strange time
Highest temperature

You should know by now
How you are
But there's no shame
In a continued dispute

It is a game
Much as I hate games
Go figure
I'm still good at it – like math
Perfectly prepared
Life is good
Don't worry, be happy.

- 2001

O.H.R.

OBSERVE - HONOR - RELEASE

OBSERVE HONOR RELEASE

THE PRACTICE THAT KEEPS ME FREE AND EASY

I have learned so many stellar lessons recently, and one of the biggest is this: there is no rush. Taking my time, moving at my own personal pace, is not just important—it's critical for the most graceful unfolding of my life. When I slow down, everything becomes clearer. I picture myself following a trail through the woods. Sometimes, the path is obvious and well-marked. Other times, it vanishes altogether. That's my cue to pause, to be still, to hang out and take in the breathtaking beauty around me. The trail will reveal itself again when it's ready. The pause is never a failure —it's a required part of the journey. And patience is not just advisable; it's essential.

When I drill down into specific lessons, they don't present themselves in a neat, linear fashion. In fact, nothing in nature is truly linear. I learned this firsthand on a 10-day vision quest near Moab, Utah in the 1990s. The experience was guided by a group trained by the Native American Ojibwe Medicine Man, author and teacher **Sun Bear,** and it completely altered how I experience nature, time, progress, and movement through life.

One of the biggest revelations came after the quest. Returning to "civilization," I struggled to do something as simple as "phone home" which required dialing a long-distance access code + the home number. Before the trip, I could have done it without hesitation. But after days "questing", of deep immersion in nature, my brain resisted that mechanical, structured task. The mental gymnastics it took to recall that number shocked me. I was also awestruck by the physical feelings and sensation of moving in a car at forty MPH after spending so long on foot in the desert.

That experience cemented something I still believe today—our paths, our learning, our growth, are not linear. Not mine. Not yours. Not anyone's. So how do I select which topics or anecdotes or epiphanies to share? Pure intuition. A gut reaction (in case you were wondering). I am endlessly amazed by the feedback I receive on my writing. What moves people, what inspires them, what resonates—it's never predictable. I don't pretend to know what is universal wisdom and what is just my own experience, but I do know that sharing my journey is valuable. Even if only one person finds something useful, that's enough.

Writing helps me assess my own clarity, motives, and next steps. But journalling isn't for everyone. Neither is meditation, music, or sports. What works for me may not work for everyone, and that's okay. The goal isn't to find a universal path—it's to honor our own unique one.

I recently read something in David Hawkins' book ***Letting Go: The Pathway of Surrender*** that completely flipped my understanding of emotions and thoughts. I had always assumed thoughts created emotions. But Hawkins suggests it's the other way around—that our feelings generate thought patterns. That means if I can release a trapped emotion, I'm also letting go of the hundreds of thoughts that orbit around it—an idea that feels both liberating and wildly appealing

As a meditator and witness to the insane number of hamster-wheel thought loops in my head, I am willing to do just about anything to shift from a chaotic mind to something more intentional, more peaceful. So, I created a simple acronym—because the world clearly doesn't have enough of them—OHR: Observe, Honor, Release.

Instead of getting lost in my thoughts, I practice this:

1. Observe – Identify what I am feeling. Not the thoughts about it, but the actual emotion behind the thoughts.
2. Honor – Acknowledge the emotion without judgment. No pushing it away. No trying to fix it. Just let it be felt.
3. Release – Let go of the need to hold onto it. Let it dissolve, let it shift, let it move through me instead of getting stuck.

When I created the OHR (Observe, Honor, Release) acronym, I thought I had everything I needed—a simple, intuitive way to work through emotions. But I quickly realized I was missing something essential: I had no real language for what I was experiencing. Noticing a feeling was one thing, but without labels, definitions, and distinctions, the process was too vague. It was like trying to navigate with a blurry map. How could I release something I couldn't even properly identify?

Since my emotional intelligence was a bit thwarted at a young age, this is all fresh, curious, heart-pumping, and adventurous for me. I have been working with *The Emotion Code* charts and recently discovered Brené Brown's *Atlas of the Heart*. Both have been unexpectedly helpful tools, giving me language and structure for emotions I may have felt but never quite defined.

That's where both the flash cards and Brown's work became fascinating. She differentiates between things like envy and jealousy, stealthy expectations vs. mindful expectations—distinctions I had never considered before. I haven't finished reading the book yet, but I'm especially looking forward to the section on positive emotions. What does she say about awe, amusement, love, trust, wonder, curiosity, and surprise?

I'm approaching all of this in a judgment-free way—not trying to force myself to feel differently, but letting myself explore and understand without urgency. And in that process, sometimes just naming what I'm feeling—even if the label shifts later—makes all the difference.

Maybe these are the real keys: I'm not in a hurry. I'm not expecting this journey to be linear. I trust that labels are just stepping stones—not limitations. I trust that this work unfolds exactly as it's meant to. And best of all? I'm actually having a blast. Stay tuned!

Let Go
Scattered thoughts of life – love – change
Pleasantly strewn, with no attachment or fear.
Just thoughts wandering in and out,
Wondering at life and it's purpose.

At me and my space.
Tired of always taking the "safe" way.
Choosing trust.
Wanting to hook into love,
snare and share it with someone.
I ponder, what will be required of me –
with separation.
The wave of trust,
Suspended and holding.
Still no fear – anxiety – concern.

Is that – after all – the secret of life?
To let go and be tossed?
Like the molecules of water
In an ocean wave?
Like the dried leaf fallen,
driven by the wind to recycle
and be born again?
As a spring shower?
Or rose petal?
I feel tossed and driven, tugged and prodded.
Yet calm and at peace for the moment.
And moment by moment,
It shifts both mood and movement.
Affected and effecting events and people
Surrounding me still tossed and driven,
What power do I have but letting go?
To flow free, not bumping the shore,
Or captured in the dam
Of someone's design.
So now attachment to
Flow – must be let go
Bottom line, let go.

- 2001

NO
FEAR

WHERE FREEDOM LIVES

THE SACRED SPACE BETWEEN REBEL AND RULEBOOK

I was only trying to sit still—just a few quiet minutes of meditation, maybe catch a breath before the to-do list came barging back in. But instead of peace, I got a full-blown inner flash mob: the Chaperone showed up, clipboard in hand, barking orders. The Rebel stomped in next, all attitude and eye-rolls. And then came the strangest revelation of all: *I am not either of them.* I'm not the one with the rules, and I'm not the one breaking them. I'm the one watching the whole scene unfold. The one sitting in the space between. And suddenly, that space—the one I usually rush to fill—became the most important place I could possibly be.

I know the Chaperone intimately. She's part Catholic school rigor, part inner perfectionist—born in the pews and classrooms of religious authority, trained to color inside the lines, follow the rules, and never ask *why*. She also carries the imprint of my workaholic father, who believed that play was for the lazy and vacation was for the weak. Joy, unless it had a measurable ROI, was suspect.

The Chaperone inherited their legacy and took it further. She doesn't just set high standards—she weaponizes them. She whispers that rest is failure, fun is foolish, and that every gold star must be earned with blood, sweat, and overthinking. She is the no-nonsense taskmaster who insists she's just trying to help, all while suffocating my spirit one "should" at a time.

Enter the Rebel, a total skeptic. The hell-no voice. She doesn't carry a clipboard—she carries a megaphone and a lighter. If the Chaperone says, "You *should*," the Rebel retorts, "You *can't make me.*" A therapist once told me that many people are stuck in their terrible twos—the emotional version—forever. Living life in a full-body tantrum of "I don't want to and you can't make me!" with angry tears and pouty lips for dramatic flair. That pretty much nails the Rebel's vibe. Big feelings, big drama. But Margaret (same wise therapist) also gave me a lifeline when she said, "There is no black and white. There are always *at least* five options." That one line cracked open my rigid thinking. And although the Rebel doesn't always know what those five options are, she sure as hell knows she won't be choosing Option A: Obey without question.

The magic happened the moment I realized that I am neither one. I am not the voice of the Chaperone, listing demands in the name of safety. I am not the Rebel either, hellbent on autonomy at any cost. I am the space between them. The awareness that watches them both. The still point in the storm. That sliver of silence between "I should" and "You can't make me" is not just a pause— it's presence. It's where freedom lives. When I identify with one voice or the other, I'm locked into their tug-of-war. But when I sit in the middle, unattached, I start to breathe. I start to see clearly.

I used to hate the Chaperone because I thought she was trying to ruin me—force me into a tight little box labeled Acceptable Human. She was trying to make me conform, crush my creativity, completely fuck up my fun. *NO FUN HERE!* she'd shout, stomping out joy like it was a fire hazard. *WTF are you thinking?* Harsh, to say the least. She was the inner critic incarnate, the original architect of my internal surveillance system—so old, so embedded, it became practically invisible. Always on, always scanning, always reporting. She didn't just whisper shame; she manufactured urgency. The breathless pace, the "go faster, do more, never stop moving" soundtrack? That's her too. Reinforced by the outside world every second of every day. The speed of it all makes it nearly impossible to notice anything subtler—especially the quiet, sacred in-between space.

And the Rebel? Oh, please. Mostly imaginary. A Thelma-and-Louise wannabe in my head, not real life. Loud mouth, big talk, no follow-through. She'd yell, *I don't care what people think!* before stomping off—exit stage left. The truth? I cared deeply. I cared so much about what people thought that the Rebel had to exist just to give me the illusion of independence. She was the inner escape hatch. A fantasy freedom fighter, shouting from the fire escape of my subconscious, while I stayed safely seated in my perfectly accept- able cubicle. But still—she had a role. She reminded me that there *was* an escape. That maybe, just maybe, I didn't have to keep dancing for approval from a rulebook I never agreed to.

And here's where it gets even more interesting. In my brief-but-beautiful brush with Native American teachings, I learned something from Sun Bear that flipped my understanding of consciousness. He described the mind not as a single narrator, but as a council —a circle of voices, each with its own viewpoint. Picture a long table in a dimly lit boardroom, chairs filled with curious characters: the Chaperone in her pressed suit, the Rebel with her combat boots on the table, and a few others I haven't fully identified yet (the Strategist? the Dreamer? the Skeptic in round glasses?). They all get to speak, but none of them *are me.* I am the one at the head of the table—the one listening. That image changed everything. I stopped trying to shut anyone up. I just pulled up a chair and said, "Thanks for sharing. I'll take it from here."

So what happens when I stop identifying with either of them? I begin to breathe. I notice the quiet underneath the commotion—the soft hum of something wiser. The field between their ropes becomes a sanctuary, not a battleground. And in that space, I find something else entirely. A deeper voice. A truer self. Not the one who reacts, defends, performs, or rebels—but the one who simply *knows.* She doesn't carry a clipboard or a lighter. She doesn't even talk loud. She just shows up. She watches. She listens. She waits. And when she speaks, the whole damn room goes quiet—not because she demands it, but because her presence alone is enough to shift the air.

The space between isn't empty—it's sacred. It's the breath before the story, the beat before the choice. It's where clarity gathers and wisdom seeps in. And no, the voices haven't gone anywhere. The Chaperone still shows up with her rules. The Rebel still wants to light things on fire. But now, I greet them like old coworkers in a shared break-room. I nod. I listen. I take what's useful. But I don't hand them the keys. I'm the one at the head of the council table now—centered, curious, and completely uninterested in running on autopilot.

So here's the deal: I am not my rules, and I am not my rebellion. I am the one who gets to decide. And that space—*where freedom lives*

—isn't a timeout or a loophole. It's the whole damn point. It's where life actually happens. It's where I reclaim my voice, not as a reaction, but as an original. So next time one of those voices tries to hijack the show, I'll do what any good field guide traveler would: step back, breathe, and remember I've got options. At least five. Maybe more.

Freedom?
Freedom is Free Fall:
Living WITHOUT a net.
The net is illusion.
Expectation equals suffering.

Freedom is the Middle Way.
We know that space.
Detachment from the
scales of Black & White and Gray.

Freedom is Curiosity:
Open – Graceful – Kind
Unassuming and weighed
down with Compassion.

Freedom is the Pause:
Just a Moment.
Breathing Deeply.
Being Witness.

Freedom is Humor:
Shift the plain to laugh.
Opening my Gifts.
My Superpower to Lift!

Freedom is Creative:
Flowing like water
over, under, thru
Un restricted or restrained.

Freedom is Listening:
Quietly – Absorbing
Accessible – Flexible
Fun and Empty.

Freedom is Noticing:
When courage springs,
when judgement leers.
And stepping aside.

Freedom is Gratitude:
Soaring the lush open
space that is Grace
No Matter What.

Freedom is Forgiving:
The culprit, the wrongdoer,
the prisoner you're releasing is
you, silly!

Freedom is mostly Friendliness:
Kindness for me.
Alone together
In this moment
Always and forever.
Love you!

- May 2020

FIELD GUIDE RULE #1: FREEDOM STARTS FROM THE INSIDE OUT.

PULLING OUT POSITIVITY

TAN LINES & TRUTH BOMBS

So many people love tropical beach vacations. I am not one of them. I recently talked myself into visiting the Bahamas, thinking that a long-time friend—who happens to be a travel professional—would help me experience the magic others seem to find in such places. And sure, I went, I experienced, I took stunning photos. The colors of the water were unreal, the beaches whiter than white. I had a lovely time… and I also left early, never needing to go back.

When people ask me about my trip, I find myself quiet or repeating the same rehearsed line: "It's beautiful, the colors are stunning, I've never seen blues like that." All true. And yet, I was expecting more—even when I thought I wasn't expecting at all! How does that happen? I'm familiar with the phrase, "Humans are meaning-making machines." Are we also expectation-making machines? Because I swear, I did my best to go in open-minded. I wasn't looking for a "transformational" experience, a spiritual awakening, or even the best vacation ever. I just wanted to see what all the fuss was about. And yet, there I was, wandering the pristine beaches, wondering what I was doing there.

Maybe it's because I'm naturally more of a mountain-and-forest person. Maybe it's because I burn just thinking about the sun. Maybe it's because sweating while doing nothing feels like an attack on my personal comfort (unless I'm in a sauna). Or maybe, just maybe, I have a hard time admitting when something just isn't for me—especially when so many people love it. So here's my challenge: Can I tell the truth and frame it positively? Can I focus on what I learned, confirmed, or observed?

For example:

- I am so happy I experienced what the Bahamas has to offer—stunning sun, sand, and surf. Now I know for sure that I have no need to go back.

- Walking on the beach, slathered in sunscreen, covered in breezy fabric, is not my idea of fun.
- There aren't as many shells as there used to be because decades of tourists have taken them home.
- Even 70–75 degrees feels uncomfortably hot to me.
- Drinking at the pool with strangers isn't my thing. Neither is reading fiction and shifting my chair every ten minutes to chase the shade of the palapa.
- Having uninterrupted time to scroll Facebook or YouTube while getting tan lines is just not my cup of tea.

Not complaining—just clarifying. I genuinely admire the people who do enjoy this type of vacation. I respect the art of perfecting the beach day, the patience required to lounge, the ability to truly relax and soak it all in. But I also know myself well enough now to say: It's just not for me. And there's something freeing about that.

Maybe the real value of the trip wasn't in finding some newfound love for tropical vacations but in confirming what I already suspected! How often do we go through life thinking we *should* enjoy something just because it's widely adored? That *if we just did it right*, we'd have the same experience as everyone else? The trip was beautiful, and I'm grateful for the experience. AND I no longer have to wonder if I'd enjoy the whole tropical island paradise thing. I don't. And that's okay.

Isn't it interesting that it feels like a problem to simply not prefer something that most people do? If I said, "I don't like sushi," no one would think I'm complaining. They'd just nod and say, "Oh yeah, not for everyone!" But when I say, "I don't love tropical vacations," there's awkward silence—like I've rejected some universal truth about leisure and relaxation.

But what if I didn't feel the need to soften it for other people's comfort? What if I just owned it? "I don't love tropical vacations. Never have. Never will. Some people love the sun and sand, and I love forests and mountains. Ain't it beautiful how we're all wired differently?"

Boom. No guilt. No second-guessing. No need to justify or prove anything. Just truth—clean, simple, and free. Now *that* is a vacation mindset worth bringing home. 😉

Beached

and you find that your loyalties are to yourself
and you wonder why it took so long
to figure that out,
and admit it.

honesty hits you again like a wave crashing,
sea water tossing and swirling around you.
throwing up sand and confusing while it hurls
    you from one plane to another.

breathless on the beach pondering
why you didn't see it coming
there it was… a white foamy crest
peaking miles out to sea
but see you didn't

so what does it mean
besides sand in your suit?
it's uncomfortable, but bearable
no fun, but part of the experience.
that gritty feeling just doesn't seem to want to
    leave.
rinse all you want, it remains
leaving you wondering…
why didn't you see it?

not prone to excuses… unfounded
nor anxious to lay blame
it seems to be a part of the cycle
like the moon and the waves…
it was the moon after all that's responsible
for the waves, that is.

from the beginning,
what were you doing on the beach anyway??
what did you hope to find?
a "cure all" or perfect answer?
wasn't what you figured, eh?

such is life.

so what now?
the worst of the two isn't bad,
the fear is only in the mind…
or is it?
so what if it isn't!!?
what then… what if the worst possible
thing you can imagine happened right now?

such is life.

and life goes on… to coin a phrase.
the dream will happen, no matter what.
no matter what
and that's a fact jack!

- December 1991

YOUR BRAIN NEEDS "A MOMENT"

NOT EVERYTHING THAT FEELS URGENT, IS...

This morning, I was cruising down the meditation highway—top down, wind in my hair, metaphorical of course—when Lucy Love dropped a 20-minute guided track called *Love Wash*. Within seconds, I was swept into that space where love lives. The kind that glows and buzzes and vibrates around you like a force field. My brain tried to label it—unconditional, palpable, effervescent—but honestly, it felt more like easing back into a cosmic rocking chair. One that reclines not just into comfort, but into *space*.

Not just outer space. Inner space. That expansive detachment I've tasted before. It reminded me of the kind of space I notice when I drop into the rhythm of this:

I set aside everything I think I know. Everything I believe to be true. All my expectations and judgments. I set aside proving, defending, looking good, and being right. All this in exchange for an open mind and a new experience of life.

That morning, I didn't say the prayer, but the feeling matched. I was off the launchpad. No gravity. That rocking chair wasn't just comfortable—it was a cosmic recliner, easing me into orbit. Spacious, weightless, no agenda. Just curiosity and the hush of something holy.

So I'm gathering visual cues to get me there on demand. The flick of a light switch—click, glow. The feeling of rose-colored glasses settling on my nose—weightless but definite—and realizing how the same scene softens through the tint of rose detachment. It's not denial. It's grace. Then there's the hidden room behind the wall of my everyday life. I stumble backward—accidentally, naturally— and land in a quiet hallway that feels like it's always been waiting. At the end? A two-way mirror. Or is it one-way? Either way, it lets me watch the whole scene unfold without having to leap into the fray. Just me, the moment, and the miracle of not reacting.

Michael Singer (author of **The Untethered Soul** and weekly **The Michael Singer Podcast**) likes to remind us we're specks on a spinning planet, careening through space. Which, yes, is helpful when you're stuck in a traffic jam or fighting with a microwave. But I wanted something more immediate. Something I could *feel*, not just *know*. A mental zoom-out is nice, but sometimes you need a full-body portal. Like, "Beam me up outta this reaction before I do something dumb." That's where the fly came in.

How about being a fly on the ceiling? Or sitting next to one? That's a fun visual. Because while my body is on the floor—flinching, vibrating, overpacked with emotion—my spirit floats up and joins that fly. And from there, I can breathe. From there, I see my life from the edge instead of the center. Not to escape, but to *observe*. That fly's-eye view? Weirdly freeing. It's the same detachment Singer points to, just closer. Smaller. With wings.

That kind of freedom would've been helpful when I almost lost my mind over a car insurance email. Let me back up. I recently bought my midlife fantasy car—a cherry red BMW convertible, the M440x iDrive. Configured it online. Picked it up. Swooned. It hugs curves, grumbles like a tiger, and makes every drive feel like a celebration. It's the kind of purchase you save for, fantasize about, and then… insure. Which, apparently, is where joy goes to die.

My agent, Robert, found me a better rate, set the switch date, and all was well. Until I opened my inbox and found a $700 invoice from the old provider. In that moment, I lost it. Snapped a pic of the email. Sent an all-caps text to Robert. Then opened a new tab to write a carefully crafted email to his boss, complete with customer service training recommendations and a few polite-but-pointed zingers.

That's when the inside voice—the intuitive warning, that hint of "you're about to make a fool of yourself"—whispered: *Wait.* So I did. Barely. I sat on my email, still fully convinced I was right, helpful, and maybe even noble in my outrage. Then Robert called. Calm as ever. Turns out the invoice had gone out before he canceled the policy, and I'd actually be getting a refund. The drama? All mine.

What saved me wasn't logic or virtue—it was the pause. It was that tiny gap where I remembered to listen instead of launch. Had I floated up to sit with the fly or ducked behind that mirror, I would've seen the story I was writing—and realized I had the pen. The power's not just in the pause. It's in the space I *create* when I stop trying to be right and remember to be free.

So I'm collecting imagery now. A rocking chair that leans into the cosmos—equal parts therapy and space travel. A spirit-fly with front-row seats to my unraveling. A switch that flips the scene from chaos to clarity. Rose-tinted glasses that turn judgments into curiosities. A secret passageway, tucked just behind the drywall of my daily panic. A mirror that says, "You don't have to fix this—you can just *see* it." And a convertible that reminds me: joy is not something to earn—it's something to choose. Preferably with the top down and the volume up. Whatever visual helps me wake up and shift, I'll take it. Because this life is for freedom. And freedom starts in the space I remember to create.

Owl, Angel or Ancestor?
Who will tell myself
about myself?
You?
The owl?
The angel?
The ancestor?
The inside voice, which one?
The wise serene one?
The brash impatient one?
The cautious thoughtful one?

Who will re-mind me?
Who will press pause?
Whose small index finger
pressures the button, pushes it down?
Sees and, AWAKE, responds

by gently pressing the PAUSE button.

Who are you?
Where do YOU come from?
and when? and how?

Never mind, never mind, never mind!
It doesn't matter.
Many thanks. I appreciate you.
I enjoy your company.
You are WELCOME.
Come around more often, whenever!
All the time – pull up a chair stay awhile.
Push my buttons anytime!
I love you!

"I love you more!"

- July 2021

LET
GO

FINDING NORTH IN A PILE OF QUOTES

PRINT IT. LAMINATE IT. LIVE IT.

There's a moment—sometimes sudden, sometimes creeping—when sadness settles over me like fog. I used to sprint in the opposite direction. Distraction? Yes, please. Denial? Absolutely. But now, more often than not, I sit down right in the middle of it. Not because I'm some emotionally enlightened nun (please), but because I've learned that feeling is how I find my way. And meditation? That's how I listen.

Don't get me wrong—I still like my peace with a side of attitude. Meditation for me isn't some floating-on-a-cloud, cue-the-chimes situation. It's more like: sit your butt down, breathe, and see what shows up. Rage, grief, relief, the grocery list—it all gets a seat at the table.

I started collecting quotes and poems during meditations—phrases that made something inside me say *yes*. Sometimes I'd type them up and make them look cute in Canva, print them on cardstock, laminate them like a nerd, and tape them to the bathroom mirror. What? Inspiration deserves a little sparkle.

Some of these lines hit so deep I read them daily for weeks. Then I shared them with friends, and the conversations they sparked helped me integrate the wisdom into my day-to-day brain static. First I heard them, then I ran like hell with them until they were beat into my bones.

These aren't just pretty words. They are survival tools. Gut checks. Gentle punches to the soul reminding me: it's okay to feel. It's not only okay—it's *the way through*. And when I'm mid-meltdown, it's often these phrases that crack the door back open to breath, to presence, to myself.

So here are some of my go-to grief-and-glory quotes. My laminated little lifesavers. May they hug you, gut-punch you, or gently dropkick you back into your own knowing.

The Guest House
This being human is a guest house.
Every morning a new arrival.
A joy, a depression, a meanness,
some momentary awareness comes
as an unexpected visitor.
Welcome and entertain them all!
Even if they are a crowd of sorrows,
who violently sweep your house
empty of its furniture,
still, treat each guest honorably.
He may be clearing you out
for some new delight.
The dark thought, the shame, the
    malice—
meet them at the door laughing and invite
    them in.
Be grateful for whatever comes
because each has been sent
as a guide from beyond.
— *Rumi*

Do not feel lonely—
the entire Universe is inside you.
— *Rumi*

These pains you feel are messengers.
Listen to them.
— *Rumi*

It's your road and yours alone.
Others may walk it with you,
but no one can walk it for you.
— *Rumi*

Letters To A Young Poet

Be patient toward all that is unsolved in your heart and try to love the questions themselves, like locked rooms and like books that are now written in a very foreign tongue. Do not now seek the answers, which cannot be given you because you would not be able to live them. And the point is, to live everything. Live the questions now. Perhaps you will then gradually, without noticing it, live along some distant day into the answer.

— ***Rainer Maria Rilke***

Let everything happen to you.
Beauty and terror.
Just keep going.
No feeling is final.

— ***Rainer Maria Rilke***

In Irish, when you talk about emotion, you don't say, "I'm sad." You'd say, "Sadness is on me." And I love that because there's an implication of not identifying yourself with the emotion fully. I am not sad—it's just that sadness is on me for a while. Something else will be on me another time and that's a good thing to recognize.

— ***Pádraig Ó Tuama***

Do not try to save the whole world or do anything grandiose. Instead, create a clearing in the dense forest of your life and wait there patiently, until the song that is your life falls into your own cupped hands and you recognize and greet it. Only then will you know how to give yourself to this world so worthy of rescue.

— ***Martha Postlewaite***

You who let yourselves feel:
> enter the breathing that is more than your own.
> Let it brush your cheeks as it divides and rejoins behind you.
> Blessed ones, whole ones, you where the heart begins:
> You are the bow that shoots the arrows and you are the target.
> Fear not the pain.
> Let its weight fall back into the earth;
> for heavy are the mountains, heavy the seas.
> The trees you planted in childhood have grown too heavy.
> You cannot bring them along.
> Give yourselves to the air, to what you cannot hold.
> — ***Rainer Maria Rilke***

These words have walked with me like soul-sidekicks in stretchy pants. I've read them aloud in tears, whispered them in meditations, printed them out and stuck them in coat pockets like secret weapons. They've become my internal playlist on the days when life gets... loud.

This isn't some curated healing aesthetic. This is me ugly-crying into my tea and remembering Rilke said no feeling is final. It's me laying down in the middle of the living room, hand on my heart, saying: "Alright sadness, you're on me. Pull up a chair." It's not fancy —but it works.

Feeling isn't a flaw. It's the flashlight. Meditation is just the quiet corner where I remember to switch it on. These words, this practice —they keep helping me find my way back. And every time I do? I cross that little inner bridge with a deeper breath, a clearer heart, and probably a new quote to laminate.

PART THREE
MAJOR FLORA & FAUNA
MENTAL JUNGLE. MEET MACHETE.

A tour of the tangled terrain inside your head—mental loops, internalized nonsense, stubborn logic, and clever self-sabotage.

This is where the mind gets wild. Expect overgrown thought patterns, circular reasoning, and the clever critters of control and judgment. Here live the ruts and rules we didn't know we were following, the coping strategies disguised as logic, and the overthinking that feels like productivity but rarely leads to peace. In this section, we track the terrain of our mental habits—our shoulds, sneaky justifications, and inner prosecutors. You'll meet manipulation, misplaced loyalty, perfectionism, and even your long-lost Watchdog. Don't worry—these aren't monsters. They're well-trained mental fauna doing their job a little *too* well. And the flora? Flowers of hope and grace blooming right alongside invasive vines of limiting beliefs and cultural bullshit. Bring snacks—and maybe a machete to hack through the thicket of thoughts.

Thought
Loops
(Top View)
defend
document
judge
satend
search
worry
worry
analyze
analyze
worry
replay
resent
resent
replay
deflect
analyze
angry
replay
deny
Spinning
Thought
Hamster Wheels
(Side View)
fear
don't
like
Thought
grooves/ruts
(Side View)

LOOPS & RUTS

SACRED GROOVES &
THE WISDOM BENEATH

I created this drawing right after a meditation on December 29, 2024. For months, I've resisted sharing it, half convinced I'd find a better way to make it self-explanatory or artistically bold. At one point, I darkened the smaller corner sketches and enlarged the wheels and ruts for clarity. Then I realized—maybe it doesn't need more polish. Maybe "you get the idea" is good enough. Because let's face it: the moment we start trying to explain our own brains, it gets messy. Mine, clearly, is a bit of a hamster circus.

That same week, an image I'd bookmarked online resurfaced in my memory: the Burren in County Clare, Ireland. Burren comes from *boíreann*, meaning "a stony place" in Irish, and when I visited last summer with Val, I was mesmerized by its cracked limestone terrain. The deep crevices, known as *grikes*, slice through the pavement like scars—and yet, life grows there. Delicate bursts of color bloom in the grikes, their roots somehow thriving in the gaps. I snapped a photo of a particularly vibrant patch, flowers blooming defiantly in the craggy rock. That image stuck with me.

As I revisited my drawing, the Burren returned—not just as memory, but as metaphor. If I were more practiced at drawing, I'd sketch the brain as its own Burren: folds of thought and memory carved with winding grikes, dotted with rogue hamster wheels spinning off in all directions. I pictured myself leaping from wheel to wheel, avoiding the slow crawl across a single rut. Because let's be honest—sometimes my inner landscape feels less like Zen and more like *American Ninja Warrior*.

Still, it captured the experience I've had countless times: repetitive, ineffective mental analysis. You know the kind. The topic loops endlessly, the ruts deepen with each lap, and before long, the same grooves are firing like bad pop lyrics on repeat. I'm not solving anything—I'm just spinning. Trying to analyze my way out of discomfort, to logic my way toward peace. And spoiler alert: it never works.

What struck me, though, as I looked at the drawing with the Burren in mind, was how neutral it all felt. There was no shame in the spinning, no blame in the ruts. The grikes weren't flaws; they were terrain. They just *were*. And in that was a surprising kind of grace. I didn't need to fix or escape them. I could, instead, learn to walk them with curiosity.

And what if—hear me out—I stopped trying to *fill* the grikes? What if, instead, I planted something in them? Not metaphorical quick-fixes, but real growth. What if those grooves could become spaces for wildflowers—unexpected pockets of color, compassion, or insight? Maybe the wheels would stop spinning long enough for me to notice the beauty blooming in the cracks.

I've often described my thought spirals to friends as "spinning," and they always nod in instant recognition. We've all done it—fixating, analyzing, rehashing. Stuck in a rut? More like stuck in a rut *with stadium seating*. But when I imagine the Burren, that language feels limiting. I like "grike" better. It feels more alive, more nuanced. And the sections of stone between the grikes? Those are called *clints*. Isn't that fantastic? The whole landscape has this living, breathing vocabulary. It makes me want to rename my neural pathways entirely. Clints and grikes, wheels and wildflowers. So much more dynamic than "rumination," don't you think?

These grooves aren't static, after all. They're shaped by what I've lived, what I've feared, what I've tried (and failed) to fix. They hold history, yes—but also possibility. The very patterns that once held me stuck might also be the ground where something new takes root. And I don't need to bulldoze the entire field to find freedom. I can start by noticing where I am, right now, and softening toward it.

I don't always know how to get out of a thought loop, but I'm learning to recognize when I'm in one. That's progress. Sometimes I pause. Sometimes I laugh. Sometimes I phone a friend and say, "I'm spinning again," and we both sigh. That alone shifts the pattern. Not with force, but with acknowledgment. With presence. It's not about perfection—it's about *practice*.

So for now, I'm letting the wheels spin and the grikes deepen, trusting that when the time is right, I'll know what to do next. Maybe I'll fill some in. Maybe I'll plant something. Or maybe I'll just sit on a clint and rest. There's no rush. No rescue mission. Just me, my funky little brainscape, and the question: what might bloom here?

That's the thing about the Burren. From a distance, it looks barren, hostile, even bleak. But if you get close—if you really *look*—there's life in the cracks. Not in spite of them, but because of them. Roots reach down into the unseen, drawing sustenance from what the eye can't detect. It's not perfect. It's not symmetrical. But it's astonishingly alive.

And maybe, just maybe, the same is true for my mind. Maybe the very places I once saw as broken or stuck are simply *becoming*. Not obstacles to overcome, but landscapes to explore. Ruts as invitations. Grikes as gardens. Wheels as reminders that I've been here before and still survived.

So I'll witness it. I'll let it be art and evidence. I'll share the drawing, even if it's imperfect. I'll show the photo, even if the light wasn't ideal. Because those flowers? They were *actually* blooming in the grike when I stood there. That part isn't a metaphor. It's proof. And maybe that's enough.

Like Really!
When you really,
Like REALLY – get it
That you are SAFE
No matter what
Happens
Nothing can hurt you.

When you really,
Like REALLY – get it,
That the universe
Protects you, loves
And Guides you,
Nothing is wrong, here – ever

When you stand
In your shoes
And make choices
And realize
Every choice is "right"
Just because.

When you really,
Like REALLY – get it
You talk
And space vibrates
You walk
And earth trembles.

Or nothing happens
And there's beauty
In nothing
Cause you're awake
When you really,
Like REALLY – get it.

When you watch
People and
Goodness is present
In EVERYONE.
Spirit shines
In smiles and frowns.

When the weather
Is "perfect" always
And "bad", "good"
"Should" and "have to"
No longer slip
From your lips.

When you really,

Like REALLY – get it
Freedom is
Love is
Now – no threats
No fears, no kidding.

And you pray
For what - ?
What you need?
It's provided w/o asking
What you want?
Who cares? So what?

When you pray you
Ask Awareness
For awareness
That all is "right" now
When you really
Like REALLY – get it.

- 1998

Manipulation!?!
LMc
10·29·24

VICE GRIP TO VELVET GLOVE

TRADING CONTROL FOR COMPASSION

How did I not see this sooner? Today's message arrived like a foghorn in a cathedral—loud, clear, and reverberating with truth. It cut through years of self-improvement schemes and sugar-free illusions. I've been watching my thoughts, policing my behaviors… but I missed the main act entirely: my motives. The hidden strings behind every "healthy" choice I make for this body.

Take weight loss. Fine. But *how* I pursue it is only the opening act. The real story? *Why* I do it. That's where the plot twist lives. Today's realization stopped me mid-scroll: my motives weren't rooted in health, or self-respect, or even kindness. They were fueled by vanity, by a desperate itch for approval, by a longing to blend in and avoid judgment. Somewhere along the way, I became a master of disguise, camouflaging my true self to pass inspection.

I once did a brutal cleanse—not to nurture my gut flora or invite healing, but because I was terrified I'd never feel good again. Fear, not love. I quit drinking to earn my partner's praise. I quit smoking because I was hacking up my dignity every morning. Not one of these decisions was rooted in reverence. They were acts of desperation. Power grabs disguised as wellness plans.

My approach has been all vice grips and boot camp. I've thrown intense rules, shame-drenched discipline, and cold control at this body, like it was a broken appliance rather than a living organism. But this job? This job needs kid gloves. Maybe a soft towel and some chamomile tea. This isn't factory work—it's sacred restoration. Holy shit, Sherlock. All my body has ever known of me is a drill sergeant with a spreadsheet and a superiority complex.

During meditation, I saw it so clearly—this gleaming metal vice grip, dripping blood and tears. My grip. My rules. My control. And still, my body endures. It's absurdly loyal, still offering energy and support despite the abuse. Somehow, it's eager for a new kind of care. A different kind of friendship. I'm ready. I'm redoubling my commitment to become the gentle caretaker my body has deserved all along. Less Marine Corps, more Montessori. Less punishment, more patience. A body isn't a problem to solve—it's a companion to nurture. Lately, I've been leaning on a handful of mantras. Tiny phrases, but they hit like soul CPR:

There is nothing to fear.
There is nothing to prove.
There is nothing to fix.
There is nothing wrong.
There is nothing missing.

They feel like the opposite of the vice grip—soft but solid, a kind of scaffolding for sanity.

"Nothing to fear" reminds me that life is generally safe, and fear? Mostly just costumes and False Evidence Appearing Real. "Nothing to prove" asks me to drop the trophy chase, to stop dancing for invisible judges. "Nothing to fix" tells me to quit hijacking other people's messes—and my own. Spoiler: it's probably not mine to solve. And "nothing missing"? That one feels like a warm blanket on a cold morning. It says, "You're whole. Even now."

Each mantra whispers its own invitation: step back, soften the grip, trust the unfolding. They guide me away from the noise of *doing* and toward the stillness of *being*. With every repetition, I feel the tension unwind. I remember what friendship with myself might actually look like.

Can I forgive myself for being a manipulator in my own body's life? For using punishment as a tool? For trying to scrub away my messiness instead of loving it clean? That's the question now. That's the practice.

And here's the kicker: it's not about never slipping back into control mode. It's about noticing faster. Loving sooner. Swapping the whip for a watering can. Letting healing take its damn time, like sourdough or wildflowers.

So no, I don't need another food plan or spiritual hustle. What I need is internal alignment. The kind that says: "You don't owe anyone anything except your own wholeness." My body's been through some things—bless it. It's still here. Still willing. And I trust it enough now to listen instead of lecture.

All is well. And this time, I'm not bracing for failure or angling for approval. I'm not recruiting allies or plotting milestones. I'm just walking beside this beautiful, resilient, wise body—and finally, finally letting it lead.

Wreckage Reclaimed –
Part 1: The Break
A trigger pulls
and something bursts open—
a million pieces flying,
shrapnel exploding—
ZING! BOOM! OOOMPH!

Landed. Ripped asunder.
Torn and bloody,
I stagger—
stunned, surprised,
shocked into silence.

Still absorbing the seismic wave,
ears ringing, speechless.
Reeling, as I struggle
to process,
to set the break,
to bind the wound,
to stitch the gash.

The world moves on,
oblivious to my carnage.
Uncaring.

Dazed and confused,
I careen forward—
sometimes lashing out,
more often piling on body armor
while musing, obsessing,
preoccupied
with planning my counterattack.

Throbbing,
finally giving up
and breaking down,
I wonder: *How?*
How can friends—family—humans
possibly be so
mindless and cruel?

Haunted by the torment,
I spin and twist,
blame myself,
blame God,
and bury the memory—
digging holes
to hide the pain completely—
until…

The next conversation spark
ignites. Goes BANG.
Rips off the scabs,
douses the mutilations
with salt.

Hopeless and hemorrhaging,
I hear the wind whisper:

"Please pause. Please remember—
You are safe.
Nothing can truly hurt or wound you.
Please remember:
I Love You.
The Illusion is just that—an illusion.
Only resistance creates suffering.
Only obsession makes it feel real."

"You—Lovely Being of Light and Grace—
do not need armor.
Do not need to numb.
Do not need to compare, control,
engage, or defend.
Resistance is useless.

Only trust. Surrender.
Breathe and remember:
You are safe and loved—
today, this day, and always."

———

**Wreckage Reclaimed -
Part 2: The Soften**
Asunder, torn asunder.
Reeling, writhing,
twisted and bleeding—again.
Life is, indeed, a hornet's nest,
a minefield, thinly veiled.

Whether I planted the ordnance
or someone else
set it under my toes…
Whether it's real or imagined,
confirmed or verified—
makes zero difference.

It matters not at all
to my ruptured heart.
I am shredded.
Staggered
Spinning. Again.

The pain is real.
Not a ruse,
Not a bad dream I'll shake off.
The seismic waves roll on.
Ears ringing. Trembling limbs.
Recovery feels like retreat.
But now I know:
Resistance is futile.

Counterattack. Avoidance.
Numbing. Defending
Even "talking it out"
or "turning to service"
Unproductive - even harmful
The pain burrows deeper still.
It covers the pressure plate
with a thin layer of soil,
where it waits to detonate—again.

Every workaround with no relief.
Every fix, a future explosion.
The hole in my heart itself whispers:

"Lovely being of light and grace,
lean in—turn toward the blast.
Breathe. Soften.
Let the emotion rush in
and flow through and
around your tender center.
FEEL Don't flee. Don't freeze.

"Forgiveness—not fear—
will temper your restless opponent.
Soften. Again.
Soften. Still.
Open the door.
Let the nightmare speak.
Show it to the light."

"Mercy will bring peace.
And gratitude,
Be grateful you are able to feel,
it is your freedom.

"This too shall pass.
You are safe.
You are loved.
Today.
And always."

- April 2021

JAN FEB MAR
1 2 3 4 5 6
8 9 10 11 12 13 22
15 16 17 18 19 26
22 23 24 25 26
$
$
$

I CAME. I PLANNED. I LAUGHED

THE FISHERMAN WAS RIGHT

The Mexican Fisherman

I don't understand or even need to know the science behind a new moon and a new month. I know the feeling and I make the connection. I awoke this morning free and clear. Like a weight that you have carried so long you forget it's there—then you notice lightness because it is gone. I had noticed the heavy feeling lately, the soreness, the lack of energy, not from anything food related—just an intensity. I celebrated 8 years sober this month. My anniversary month is sometimes heavy... not sure why that is, but other sober people experience a certain oddness to their anniversary time.

Anyway... I feel better. Bottom line. And I have some fun things to share.

I decided to get out in the sunshine yesterday (vitamin D could be it?) and finish reading a book for a "book club"—***Four Thousand Weeks: Time Management for Mortals*** by Oliver Burkeman. I had to refresh myself by reading the notes and comments and highlights from the first part. Then I started reading Part 2 – Beyond Control. And then—this gem:

The Parable of the New York Businessman and the Mexican Fisherman

An American investment banker was at the pier of a small coastal Mexican village when a small boat with just one fisherman docked. Inside the small boat were several large fin tuna. The American complimented the Mexican on the quality of his fish and asked how long it took to catch them.

The Mexican replied, "Only a little while."

The American then asked why he didn't stay out longer and catch more fish.

———

Excellent, yes?! A perfect parable in its own right, and a perfect mirror to hold up to our modern madness.

The book does a great job describing the cultural bonds we inherited from the Industrial Age—being paid by the hour, judging time as either productive or wasted, using our calendars and task apps like tiny control panels to micromanage a future that will *never* bend to our will. But what I love is that Burkeman doesn't preach. He just points out the unspoken nonsense we all live by, consciously or unconsciously. And that is enough.

This parable, in particular, hit hard. It encouraged me to pause and look at *what do I love to do?* Not what I should do. Not what I might do next. Not what will help me earn approval or maintain appearances.

What would I actually choose—if nobody was looking?

Now that I'm retired, I don't HAVE to volunteer, or teach, or study, or exercise, or walk, or do a single thing to justify my existence. I've done plenty. I've earned enough gold stars to last this lifetime and maybe two others. So what now?

My new meditation intention is to just BE ME and see what that feels and looks like.

No small order, considering I've spent most of my life trying to live up to someone else's ideals, expectations, and shoulds—without even realizing they weren't mine. It's not that I was being fake. I just didn't know I had options. I didn't know I had a choice in how to spend my days, or how to *feel* my days.

Turns out: I do.

And so do you.

One of my favorite insights from the book is his playful, humble definition of a plan:

"A plan is a statement of intent, an expression of your current present moment thoughts about how you'd really like to deploy your modest influence over the future. The future, of course, is under no obligation to comply."

YES. Can we please print that on mugs, t-shirts, email footers, and strategic planning documents everywhere?

I've spent too many years pretending I had control—or trying to force it. I don't want to waste any more time ignoring or avoiding the deep truth that I never had it in the first place. Life was never meant to be wrestled to the ground and tamed. It was meant to be lived—*like the Mexican fisherman.*

So here's the plan: be me. Not some optimized, improved, impress-the-internet version—just actual me. I'll follow the spark, ignore the calendar, maybe organize a drawer or two and call it alignment. But if I've learned anything, it's this: even my best-laid plans are usually just appetizers for the universe's next joke.

That's why I've stopped making Plan A—or even B. These days I go with Plan G: *Good luck with that.* Because something weird, wonderful, or wildly inconvenient will absolutely show up instead. And somehow, that's when I learn the most. That's when I laugh, let go, and remember that control was never the goal.

Being here was.

Un-Becoming
Stand back, please!
Look away!
I'm becoming -
I'm just becoming over here.
Nothing to see.

I'll be back shortly, perhaps.
Or it may take awhile.

PLEASE DON'T STAND AROUND!
DON'T BOTHER TO WAIT, REALLY!

I'll be fine. Just becoming over here.
Nothing to see.

I get a sense that I'm becoming
what I once was.
I'm UN-BECOMING - really.
Washing, cleansing,
Peeling, scrubbing.
NOT "healing" over!
NOT covering up!

I'm simply removing some
Un-needed, un-necessary,
Add-on layers of B.S. -
All sorts...
(religious - cultural - familial - corporate -
emotional - environmental)

BULLSHIT thoughts and insane behaviors.
Illusions, delusions and drivel all can go...
      Adios!

I'll be un-becoming
for a bit
over here.

Nothing to see!
I'm doing fine!
Move along!
Don't Wait Up!

I'll be "right with you"
when I'm good and ready.
In the mean time... love you, miss you.
Be back soon.

- December 2019

ACCEPT
ENJOY
ENTHUZE

AE²: ACCEPT, ENJOY, ENTHUSE

THE SEEKING IS OVER.
THE HONESTY BEGINS

This will be a quickie, ladies and gents. I am declaring the season open again. The pendulum has swung back. The tide is in for writing. The docks are high and even, and they are accepting incoming ships and boats and visitors.

I am a seeker no longer. This is new as of a few months ago. I could pinpoint the day and time, the epiphany, the event—but there's no need. Suffice it to say that I now declare: I am no longer adrift in a hunt for something or someone to complete me, inform me, or save me.

There is much more to this shift—layers I may wish to explore or share in time. But for now, what matters is that the shift is real. It is still settling in, still sinking into my skin, and in doing so, it is exposing all sorts of dusty corners I hadn't seen before. Patterns of thought, subtle behaviors, reactive loops I didn't even register as "searching"... now they glow neon.

Because now that the soul is revealed and the search is over, the habits of the hunter keep showing up anyway. They swarm in like mosquitoes at dusk—subtle at first, then suddenly everywhere, leaving you itchy, agitated, and reaching for something to make it stop. Sometimes it's a flare of urgency. Sometimes it's a stray twinge of envy. Or a random impulse to Google something, buy something, text someone. My favorite surprises are the subtle ones—a longing tucked inside a compliment, a flicker of resentment hiding behind helpfulness.

I'm not scouring the map anymore—but I *am* noticing more than ever. What fun. This is the true adventure: discovery without the compulsion to seek. A paradox, of course. Which is, in my experience, the best terrain for spotting truth.

I am still inquisitive. Still curious. Still adventurous. Let's be clear—I'm not numb or settled or satisfied in some bland, smug, "got it all figured out" way. But I am no longer the mindless, frantic seeker endlessly peeling onions, hoping the core will reveal a radiant golden answer. The onion doesn't need peeling. It's already whole. Comfortable and whole. Nothing to fix. Nothing to chase.

I've said this aloud a few times now—mentioned to a few friends that I am no longer on a quest. The responses have ranged from aghast concern for my soul and sanity to complete apathy. I haven't yet come across someone who nods and says, "Ah yes, the hunger has stilled. Me too." That's okay. I might not be explaining it well. Which is probably why I'm writing this down: clarity often reveals herself only when I force my brain to put words in a row.

So let me be clear: the crusade I have abandoned—and continue to remind myself I have abandoned, and continue to be enlightened by the abandonment of—is this: the belief that I'm missing something, that I'm not enough, and that someone out there has the missing bit. The imagined fix. The final word. I still need people—of course I do. For reflection. For friendship. For triggering my blind spots and sharpening my edges. But I don't need anyone else to complete my connection to the Unseen. That relationship is already intact. Sometimes it just needs my attention.

The mind and ego still ask their questions—questions that have no answers. And the old wiring still occasionally imagines those answers might be Out There: in the right book, the right guru, the right wind or tarot card. But I know better now. Silly girl. No shame. That compulsion got me here. But once you see the mechanism clearly, it's hard to unsee.

So what's left when the hunt is over? Presence. But not the dreamy, sit-on-a-cushion presence that gets sold like some kind of spa product. I'm talking about fierce presence. Noticing when I'm even slightly out of alignment. Watching for the red flags. You know the ones: irritability, restlessness, and discontent. The holy trinity of emotional static. If I'm feeling off—defensive, snappy, impatient, smug, dismissive, indignant, low-grade cranky—I know I've stepped out of myself and into the noise.

The good news? That's the cue. That's my reminder to shift

back. I'm experimenting now with just a single brilliant idea from *A New Earth* by Eckhart Tolle, three states of awakened doing: Acceptance, Enjoyment, and Enthusiasm. AE². Like a formula. Like a map—not for where I'm going, but for how I want to move through whatever this is.

If I can't genuinely *enjoy* the moment I'm in, can I at least *accept* it? Like changing a tire in the rain—wet, cold, mildly miserable, but necessary. The resistance adds suffering. The moment you stop arguing with the rain and start moving with purpose, there's relief. Acceptance doesn't mean you love it. It means you're not wasting energy resenting the fact that it's happening (or happened already… year ago?!)

Other times, joy sneaks in. Unexpectedly. I find myself smiling while folding laundry or giggling at how mad I am that the grocery store rearranged their aisles again. That's *enjoyment*. And it changes everything.

Enthusiasm, as Tolle describes it, is the rare and radiant flow-state that rises when you're aligned with a deeper purpose. It's not manic or egoic. It's a quiet surge. A wave that sweeps you up, moves you through the task, and then gently sets you down when the thing is complete. You can't manufacture it. But when it arrives—follow it.

So now, instead of reacting, I'm experimenting. Practicing. Fiercely. Each time I notice I'm triggered or tight, I pause. I try on one of the three hats: Can I accept this? Can I enjoy this? Am I feeling enthusiastic about this? If not, maybe I'm in resistance. Maybe I'm clinging to control. Maybe it's just an old story trying to sneak back in.

And here's a new one I've been playing with: If you spot it, you got it. If something bugs me—a person, a situation, a tone, a choice —I pause and ask: What about this is annoying me? And is that trait... maybe... lurking in me too? It usually is. It's not punishment —it's curriculum. Life shows me my own residue, one triggered moment at a time. *Stay tuned—this one deserves its own trail marker.* Same goes for paradox: if something feels upside down and strangely true, that's probably the truth waving a flare gun. *More on that later too.*

So no, I'm not on a quest anymore. But I am deep in the prac-tice. Not seeking. Not fixing. Just noticing. And choosing, moment by moment, to respond from one of three places: Acceptance. Enjoyment. Enthusiasm. Because if it doesn't fall into one of those three? It's probably just another bloodsucker buzzing in my brain. And I'm done feeding that swarm.

Sick?
Are you un-well?
Are you dis-eased?
out of order?
Perhaps you are
ailing? or ill?
Afflicted with the
expectation of suffering?
but are you sick?
truly? ever?

Does someone
"out there"
have your cure
your miracle?
Perhaps your God
will re-pair you?
The 12 Steps will
they re-store you?
What magic sauce
will salve and set you "right"?

Surely you must hunt
And seek and
struggle as you suffer
and clash and combat
your sickness
that you don't deserve
and didn't ask for.
Surely life owes
you serenity
and wellness!

And so you are off…
to the races
chasing your tail
or your hare.
Silly girl!
You are not unwell.
You are not diseased,
ailing, ill or afflicted.
You need no-one
and no-thing to save you.

Patience will provide.
Awareness will shift.
Trust will transform.
The paradox of pure
Detachment & Oneness
will unveil and reveal
the beauty, purpose and
ever-present wisdom that IS.
BE, Love, Breathe.
All is well!

- September 2020

HOLY SCHMOLY, IT'S JUST MY BODY

BUILT BY NATURE, FUELED BY WONDER

"Your body is a temple." "You should treat your body like a temple." This is an old saying, one I remember hearing occasionally from the time I was very young. I understand the idea of it—to treat your body as sacred and holy. But no one in my immediate family was a living example of this, so I can't remember ever taking this platitude very seriously.

I distanced myself from religion pretty much as soon as I was emancipated—able to vote, live on my own and make choices for myself without the watchful oversight of a parent. This distance applied to anything and everything related to Catholicism or Christianity in general and extended to the places of worship too, now that I think of it. I was in a church for the first time in decades on my trip to Iceland and Ireland. The building in my image is the the Evangelical-Lutheran church Hallgrimskirkja in the center of Reykjavík.

During a recent BYOB (Be Your Own Bestie) meditation, the image of a temple—very similar to the one I saw in Reykjavik—appeared with a big X over it, clear as a bell. Interesting, I thought, how resistance, guilt, and who knows how many other negative associations with religion and religious buildings had apparently bled over into my own caring concern for my body. There was an instant acceptance: my body is not a temple. Another shortsighted, culturally acceptable dictum bites the dust!

A temple is man-made, it has absolutely nothing to do with my 100% natural physical being. A temple is built according to a blueprint, designed with structure and rules. But my body? My body wasn't designed by a committee. It wasn't planned with symmetry and stone, laws and liturgy. My body grows, shifts, regenerates, breaks down, and rebuilds. It is genius, organic, unpredictable, fluid —nothing like a fixed, sacred structure built by men to be admired but not truly lived in.

It struck me how deeply this resistance had embedded itself. Had I, without realizing it, internalized the idea that caring for my body came with so much baggage? That if I wasn't treating it a certain way, I was somehow sinful? The guilt of religious obligation had shape-shifted into a quiet, nagging, "should spouting" voice about my health, my choices, my physical self. No wonder the image of the temple with an X appeared—my subconscious had been waiting for permission to reject the comparison outright. My body is not a temple.

My body is my home. A temple is a place people visit, a destination, something separate from daily life. My body is my home. I don't visit it—I live in it. It holds me, moves me, teaches me. It has been with me through thick and thin, unselfishly carrying me forward. Always giving 1000%. I have never been truly alone—my body has been here, steady, present, enduring. Like any home, it needs tending, repair, rest. It is both a mystery and something deeply familiar, cozy and safe, even as it shifts and changes with time. It's not here to be worshiped or placed on a pedestal—it's here to be appreciated, inhabited, fully and enjoyed freely.

My body is my playground, full of adventure and experiences of all sorts. A playground made for exploration, for running, jumping, feeling the rush of motion and sensation. My body gives me access to experiences—the smell of earth, the sensation of the sun and wind on my skin, the stretch of muscles waking up in the morning. It lets me move, dance, taste, feel. Why would I not delight in all the joy this planet has to offer? Why would I not partake with enthusiasm in living this precious life to it's fullest potential.

My body is my garden, alive and growing, shifting with the seasons of my life. Some days, it is lush and thriving, full of energy, and everything is in bloom. Other times, it needs careful pruning, weeding, observing. It doesn't follow a strict, rigid plan—it responds to the seasons of life, sun, wind, rain, attention, and nourishment. If I abandon it, it overgrows in chaos or withers in neglect. But when I tend to it, even in small ways, something beautiful always finds a way to bloom.

My body is my instrument, built for creativity, movement and expression. Some days, it hums effortlessly, attuned and resonant. Other days, it creaks and groans, needing tuning and patience. But no matter what state it's in, it holds music, waiting to be played. I do not worship it—I listen to it, work with it, and allow it to move in harmony with my life.

My body is my ocean, vast and untamed, shifting with the tides of the moon, vibrations, energy, emotion, and experience. Some days, it is calm and glassy, effortlessly flowing. Other days, it is stormy and unpredictable, demanding attention, reminding me of its depth and power. It carries me, whether I fight against it or allow myself to float. And like the ocean, it holds mysteries beyond what my conscious mind will ever fully understand.

My body is my mountain, raw and alive, untouched by rigid definitions of what it "should" be. It does not follow a linear path; it is full of twists, turns, and surprises. Some days, it is vibrant, wild, and free. Other days, it is quiet, reserved, conserving its energy. It cannot be conquered, only respected, explored, and understood.

My body is my story, written moment by moment. It is a collection of experiences, a living, breathing narrative that evolves with time. Some pages are filled with strength, others with rest. Some chapters hold struggle, while others overflow with joy. It is not meant to be perfect, only true.

I have come to know my own body as nothing short of miraculous in all its workings and abilities and functions. And I don't have to go anywhere or construct anything or consult anyone to witness this miracle. My body is a mystery beyond explanation, even if you gathered every doctor, yogi, and mystic from the beginning of time until now. Even though I am presently at peace with religion and most things religious, my body is still nothing like any temple ever built by any human or group of humans anywhere on this planet.

So no, my body is not a temple. It is not built just for worship, for quiet reverence, for rules and rituals. My body is my home, my playground, my garden, my instrument, my ocean, my wilderness, my story. It does not need holiness—it needs love, attention, movement, and trust. And that is more sacred than any temple ever built.

My Body of Wonder
Oh body, my body
I stand in awe
Struck by the beauty
Afraid to approach
Shy of the wisdom
Complexity
Perfection

You are mine
We are one
Mystery
Spirit, Mind, Body-
Trinity

No more
punching bag
No longer
whipping post

I am embarrassed
I am humbled
I am angry

Step past the anger
Past the hurtful -
Find curiosity
Timid wariness

Will you teach me
Your language
Share your wisdom?

I surrender

No longer combatant
The Spirit / Mind Gladiator
Kneels before you

My radio tuned
To this station
Trusting child
At elder's knee

Assume nothing
Remain bashful
Biddable
Respectful
And Blushing

I feel deficient
And dazzled
My body, this sleeve
Knows more than every
Doctor ever born

Astonished gratitude
And modest
Tempered
Contrite
Attention
Forth coming.

- March 2018

THE WATCHDOG SPEAKS...

TURNS OUT, MY INNER GUARD DOG HAS EXCELLENT MANNERS

Before I ever knew about inner parts work or psychological integration, I wrote this. A spontaneous poem-dialogue with the ever-alert inner voice that had been watching, protecting, and over-functioning for decades. I didn't name it "the Watchdog" right away—it named itself. This is the transcript of our first real conversation. Spoiler: It had a LOT to say.

The Watchdog Speaks
Hello there!
Hey! Hello!
Are you watching me?
Hey—hello?
What do you see
There, behind me?
To my side?
Behind my knee?
Hey, what do you see
And why are you watching me?
I've seen you here.
You've been around.
I've seen you here before.
Not sure why, it's just dawned on me
To ask you why –
Say – why are you watching me?

I know I'm not alone
In here –
I've met some of

your comrades.
In dreams
In meditations
In emergencies
and in quiet moments.
But we have not been
Introduced. What's your name, watcher?

I know you're not my witness,
My oneness or my physical frame.
I sense that you are other--
What's your name?
Keeper? Minder?

Are you the subtle, instant
Judger? The one that's
Looking out – alert – wary –
Vigilant? Keen? Cautious?
Hello there! Welcome!!
It's a pleasure
To meet you finally!

Why are you here now?
Is there something I can do?
Might I add, you're amazing?
Your talent, your skill--
Remarkable, astounding,
Many thanks for being here!

A makeover? A refresh?
An upgrade? Indeed!
We can manage that,
So happy that you know
You're out of date for me.
How shall we proceed?
What is there to do?
A brand-new education

And a new perspective too!?

Excellent timing BTW,
the game has shifted,
I see it too,
and the old way no longer works.
How shall we go about it?
Do you have a clue?
"Honest, open, willing—the same, just as
        before."

"I'm stepping up and
standing out so that you
will know – it's working,
the introspection –
another layer
going – going – gone."

Are you a poet too?
Because we've missed you.

"The poet is not me
but I can set the poet
free."

You've been on autopilot
for as long as I've been here.
Watching – scouting –
recording all there is
to FEAR.

My escort, my defender--
I'm here – NOW – because
of you.

I hear your whispered worries and
suggestions

Even now I apprehend.
Don't fret—the paper won't run out, the pen
    won't run dry.
And there's time for stickers later.
I value this conversation.
It's priceless, so helpful.
Please, don't be shy.

"Acknowledgment. Attention. Listening.
Consideration. Compassion.
Surrender. Let go!
Invite Love to observe.
Just allow release and freedom!"

Watchdog? Okay then 😉.
(And yes, you totally remind me of that
    sketchy guy from The Sketch Artist, equal
    parts detective and shadow.)
I'm beyond thrilled, so excited--
you have no idea!
A huge missing section
of my puzzle has appeared!

I know this is drastic—frightening, even—
    uncomfortable.
You're so amazing and
so lightning fast.
But how can we work together
to turn the tide?
"Patience and awareness,
Effort and creative skill.
We blow away the old
like dandelion fluff.
Invite kindness, recall safety, remember
    TRUST."

There's so much to let go of,

but I'm ready to begin anew.
Today, and every day.
"Me too!"
And just like that, we begin.

2025

STEALTH MODE OFF

SURVEILLANCE TERMINATED

I am the oldest of my siblings and cousins. First-born grandchild. All eyes were on me—until they weren't. Around age seven, my mother remarried and decided to start a second family. Enter Mark and David, born when I was nine-and-three-quarters and eleven-and-some-change. They were night and day—Mark, a bold and boisterous firecracker; David, a quiet and cautious shadow. Together? My personal pint-sized chaos committee. They tattled, pried, cried, and raided my room like it was their full-time job.

I was fourteen and "in charge" of a three- and four-year-old. At sixteen, I had a five- and six-year-old under my weary wing. I was more resentful older sister than willing stand-in parent, and by the time college loomed, I was fantasizing daily about my exit strategy. But here's what stuck: those two, in all their boundary-pushing glory, taught me how to hide. If I wanted privacy, peace, or a moment alone for any reason, it had to be covert. Mark was obvious in his mischief. David was invisible. And me? I perfected the art of getting away with things quietly, undetected. Honestly, I should've earned a merit badge.

I got so good at it, I once scaled the olive tree next to our pergola just to sneak a smoke. I'd tightrope the beams, haul myself onto the flat gravel roof of our mid-century modern house, and hide out with my cigarettes, a journal, and my Vivitar camera. It was my personal rebel retreat: above it all, alone, and free—at least until I had to quietly shimmy down again like nothing ever happened. I did this regularly, mind you. Not exactly "occasional contraband." This was a daily summer creativity exercise in stealth, privacy and pleasure. Honestly, part of me still loves how ingenious it was... but also, wow. That's a lot of effort just to find five quiet minutes, have a puff, snap a cloud photo, and avoid being observed by a duo of toddlers with loose lips.

Let's talk sneaky. Like dirty talk, but less sexy and more...

strategic dysfunction. I recently had a meditation session where my inner guidance—my DMGS—lovingly called me out (Divine Magical Guidance System). It showed me how sneaky has survived into my current life as a subtle, habitual form of self-sabotage. Not bold or dramatic, just slippery. A muttered internal *"just this once"* or *"don't mention it and maybe it won't count."* And I'm noticing: it's not just a behavior. It's a vibration.

Take the chocolate almond incident. A few nights ago, I was rummaging for a cooking tool and stumbled across a container of Trader Joe's dark chocolate covered almonds. I'm pretty damn good at hiding shit from myself, mostly! Instant trigger, sneaky activated: *Don't tell Chris. He's on a diet. I'll ration them, make them last.* Uh huh. Night one: too many almonds, bad sugar hangover. Night two: I made a show of putting some in a bowl, out in the open... but said nothing. Chris said nothing. We both knew. The energy was weird and weirdly familiar. That's what got my attention.

This wasn't about almonds. It was about access, control, and the ancient belief that if I don't hide what I want, I won't get it—or worse, I'll be judged for it. Sneaky is how I learned to survive when I didn't feel articulate enough to explain, confident enough to claim, or worthy enough to ask. It's not just about avoiding consequences. It's about preemptively disqualifying myself from authenticity.

But here's the thing: I'm turning 60 next month. I've got tools now. I've got pause, breath, awareness, and a very sassy inner guidance system. I know that when I feel that slippery sneakiness arise, I can *wait*. I can raincheck my reaction. I can trust that clarity will come. I can speak from integrity without bracing for attack. I don't need to squirrel away what I want like I'm still under surveillance. I can be honest. I can be seen. I can be free.

And while we're at it, can we talk about the invisible audience in my head? The peanut gallery of imaginary critics who seem deeply invested in how I load the dishwasher or whether I'm using enough elbow grease in the shower? Who are these people? Ghosts of judgment past? An inner panel of exasperated relatives? The worst part is, they never leave—it's more of a vague disapproval cloud, like I'm being watched by someone who's perpetually unimpressed. Even when I'm alone. Even when I'm doing something incredibly helpful, like shoveling snow so no one breaks an ankle. Apparently, my inner surveillance team isn't big on gratitude. But now that I see them clearly, I'm tempted to wave and say, "We're good here. You can go." Or better yet—hand them a clipboard and put *them* to work for a change.

Here's the connection I didn't see before: sneakiness is a response to imagined judgment. If I didn't feel like I was being watched, evaluated, or silently disapproved of—why would I need to be sneaky at all? Sneakiness only exists when there's someone to hide from, even if that someone is a dusty inner voice from the 1970's. The surveillance feeds the sneak. The sneak confirms the need for surveillance. It's a self-sustaining loop of unworthiness, and every time I act from it, I reinforce the idea that I can't be real and be safe at the same time.

But I see it now. The pattern. The payoff. The cost. I can shift it. I can pause, take a breath, and check in with my actual self—not the jury. I can move from this weird little jail of judgment and manipulation into something that feels a hell of a lot better: freedom, creativity, transparency. A kind of badass clarity that says, *I want this. I don't need permission. I trust myself.* Sneaky had its time. But this next chapter? This one's wide open. No secrets. No surveillance. Just me, free and clear.

Hide & Seek

One, two, three
four, be *present*
five, six, *breathe*
seven, *pause,*
eight, nine, *observe*
ten! Ready or not
here I come…!

"I'm NOT ready,
Five seconds more…
Please??!"

OK. ONE – get ready

TWO – be *mindful*

THREE, FOUR – you're *safe*

FIVE – be *HONEST.*

Ready or not here I come.

-Silence-

The seeking begins…
Am I seeking honesty or is it seeking me?
Am I hiding or is he?
There's a shadow…
There – did it move?
A flash of color,
A momentary glimpse.
Is that dishonesty? sneaky & hiding?
Surely it's not honesty
playing hard to get?

How am I to know for sure?
Feel my way? of course!
Tune into those internal sign posts,
nudges, jabs, prods, hunches and shoves.

I am seeking honesty so
Honesty is also seeking me!
Relax, here I am.
You've found me.

August 2020

PART FOUR
WEATHER PATTERNS

A CLIMATE GUIDE FOR THE TENDER & TEMPEST-TOSSED

Forecast: change; mood swings, emotional storm fronts, tears like rain, and breathtaking moments of stillness.

Welcome to the emotional climate zone. This is where the storms roll in, the fog thickens, and just when you think you've figured it all out—boom! Hailstorm of old grief. We're talking about mood swings, fury flare-ups, sudden clarity, and long dry spells. This section explores the emotional atmosphere we move through—how it shifts, how to ride it, and how not to get struck by lightning (metaphorically speaking). These essays won't tell you to "stay sunny." Instead, they invite you to feel what you feel and discover the kind of grounded trust that holds steady even when the skies turn dark. Spoiler: there's beauty in EVERY storm—especially the scary ones. And unlike the Wicked Witch of the West, you won't melt if you get caught in a downpour. You'll be soaked maybe, but you won't melt—and you've got miles to go, darling.

FURY
CLEANSE

THE FURY CLEANSE

ANGER ISN'T UGLY
- IT'S ALCHEMY

I've heard it said—and I believe it—that every experience has a bright side, a learning opportunity. As humans with free will, how we choose to observe and interpret each moment is one of our built-in superpowers. That said, let's be real: some emotions are sticky and stormy, unwilling to reveal their purpose, plan, or lesson. Anger, for instance. For most of my life, I've shoved it aside, numbed it out, softened the edges. Rarely do I allow myself to honor it, honestly and fearlessly.

And let me tell you—yesterday, it refused to be ignored. It wasn't just a 'weird-dream' morning crankiness—I've danced that dance. This was deeper, sharper, and harder to shake. This was insatiable. Unquenchable. I tried movement shaking and dancing it away. Still there. It clung to me like static and insisted on closer inspection. Fine. What?! *What??* And there it was. Not just anger. FURY. A tidal wave.

"I want to be thin!" it screamed.

Not politely or wistfully. Not in a wellness-goal, intention-setting, affirming kind of way. This was primal. Rageful. A red-hot eruption that cut through all my delusional bypassing. It didn't care about cultural expectations or body-positive compassion or moderate, reasonable self-talk. It did not want balance. It wanted TRUTH. And apparently, the truth was: I'm fed up.

I'm fed up with the excuses, the gentle indulgences, the soothing stories. I'm sick of being hungry, of negotiating with cravings, of pretending I'm at peace when my body is screaming for more. *It felt good to admit it. Even to hate it.* Even to hate *myself* for the never ending sabotage and inevitable spiral. I wrote furiously:

"I'm sick and tired of being HUNGRY. I don't want to be hungry ever again. FUCK you, hunger! I can't trust you. You LIE! I am not in need of anything."

What a relief. That's the power of fury—it doesn't negotiate. It slices through the noise and lays it bare. Beneath all my gentle intentions was a core truth: I'd been pretending balance and moderation were enough, but I was faking it. Something inside me knew it wasn't right—I was waiting for the shoe to drop, for old behavior to sneak back in. I couldn't detach. I was tangled in familiar patterns and wishful thinking. Fury cut through all of it like a hot knife thru butter. Brutal, yes—but brilliantly clear. My goal wasn't aligned with what my body really wanted. Fury to the rescue—who knew? Without it, I might still be fake-moderating my way through madness, AGAIN!

So I made a decision (cut off all other options, full definition below). I'm fasting. Cleansing. Just tea and water. *Nothing to fix, just a system reset.* And you'd be shocked by how *right* it feels. Everything I've done up to this point—clearing out trigger foods, hoarding detox tea (Nettle, Hibiscus, Chaga, Burdock Root, Ginger, Mango Ginger, Smooth Move, Fenugreek, Raspberry, Mullein… I could open a shop)—all of it suddenly clicked. Even aspirin made the cut. (Caffeine withdrawal is no joke.)

By the afternoon meditation time, I wasn't glowing—I was quiet. Hollowed out, in the best possible way. Not because the hunger had vanished, but because something deeper had surfaced: a decision that felt cellular. The old part of me—the excuse-maker, the gentle negotiator, the saboteur—had stepped aside (at least for the moment). Not with drama, but with a kind of weary bow. In her place was something stripped down, steady, and certain. I didn't feel triumphant. I felt emptied. Clear. Like the hunger had finally named itself, and with that truth came peace.

During that afternoon's meditation, so many thoughts drifted past like boats on a river—some familiar, some surprising. No need to chase or catalog them. But somewhere mid-stream, something different floated by—something quieter, but undeniable. I caught a glimpse of what it might mean to give away my emptiness. To surrender that vague, gnawing sense of not enough. That restless current of longing—for acknowledgement, for intimacy, for stillness—that never quite names itself, never feels fully satisfied. It was just there, bobbing gently in the flow, waiting for me to notice. A subtle shimmer beneath the surface. And I saw it. I COULD LET GO OF EMPTINESS ITSELF. I could actually turn *that* over. Let *that* go. Not fix it. Not soothe it. Not embrace or honor it. Just let it go.

And honestly? I was floored. How had I missed this? After all that searching, it turns out, this emptiness inside wasn't some sacred portal or cosmic to-do list item. It was just... noise. A drama queen with a fog machine. Hunger's shady cousin wearing a different costume. Spiritual static dressed up as deep longing. And suddenly, I didn't need to decode it or dive into it or drag it to therapy. I could just laugh, wave, and let that slippery bastard float downstream. Poof.

Fury, it turns out, is brilliant—when you let her have the mic. Not forever. Not on repeat. But for that one knockout moment of clarity? She *slaps*. She doesn't whisper affirmations or light candles —she kicks the door in, points at the truth, and dares you to deal with it. And when you do? When you *really* listen and let her burn off the bullshit? You don't just feel lighter. You are lighter.

So yeah, I'm sipping my absurd teas, giving my saboteur a well-earned nap, and leaning into this strange, radiant relief. Hunger can take a hike. Emptiness too. For now, I've got fury in my corner—and she's not here to coddle. She's here to set me free.

*Definition: decision (n.) mid-15c., decisioun, "act of deciding," from Old French décision (14c.), from Latin decisionem (nominative decisio) "a decision, settlement, agreement," noun of action from past-participle stem of decidere "to decide, determine," literally "to cut off," from de "off" (see de-) + caedere "to cut" (from PIE root *kae-id- "to strike").*

What???
When yesterday
Tomorrow and forever
Stand before me
Now
I tremble
I'm not ready
Prepared or equipped
Properly

I could be.
What it would take is
The stance of generations
The testosterone of millions
Before me to make
This creation
Reality

Rally that will you?
Question all and everything
That came before
That speaks in the moment
Rally all you are and move
Forward in spite
Spite is good and strong
Anger is a powerful tool
Much stronger than wistful wanting
or wishful thinking.

May 2001

I
U

PERMISSION GRANTED

MEDITATION, MOOD SWINGS & MESSAGES FROM THE FOG

"I love YOU!"

What a lovely message to send to myself. Not in a desperate-post-it-note-on-the-mirror kind of way, but a genuine little whisper from the inside. Simple. Sweet. Unexpected.

Today, I started a new practice: meditate, create a piece of artwork, then write about it. Nothing elaborate—just a rhythm, a ritual. A little soul whisper in three acts. This morning, I listened to a guided meditation called *Accessing Your Intuition*. During the 14-minute session, a lot of tough questions were suggested—ones I found surprisingly uncomfortable to answer in the moment.

"Notice how you feel, in this very moment."

"How do you feel physically? Mentally? Emotionally?"

Ugh. I felt heavy, thick, pissy, and grumpy. The kind of mood where even your socks feel like they're judging you. Maybe it's just hard to admit that I'm human and sometimes in a bad mood. I'm generally an eternally optimistic person—so it sucks to acknowledge when I'm not. And honestly, I've realized I really don't like being asked, "How do you feel?" It feels... intrusive. Defensive shields go up. Why are you asking? What do you want to do with my answer? Fix me? Analyze me? Use it against me later?

The meditation guide went on to describe how intuition might communicate—through feelings, visuals, sounds, words, or experiences. "Take a moment now to ask your intuition anything…"

I took a breath. I didn't expect much. But within a few short minutes, the thick pissiness lifted just enough for a visual to come through. It was clear and sweet. No lecture. No explanation.

I ♥ U

Three simple characters. No strings attached. It felt sincere. Uncomplicated. At least someone, something, loves me enough to help me let go of the funkiness, moodiness, and self-pity.

That's what meditation does for me—not every time, but often enough to keep coming back. It offers a little lift. A subtle invitation. A reminder that whatever mental weather I'm experiencing isn't the whole sky. It passes. It shifts. Sometimes it even delivers a message shaped like a glittery sticker from the Universe.

For context, the official definition of meditation according to Wikipedia is: *"a practice in which an individual uses a technique – such as mindfulness, or focusing the mind on a particular object, thought, or activity – to train attention and awareness, and achieve a mentally clear and emotionally calm and stable state."* Yeah…that. Also known as: trying not to strangle someone before coffee.

I didn't start out meditating for 20 minutes on a fancy cushion in silence with incense and wind chimes. No. I started with two minutes. Just two. For 30 days. Then 60. Then 90. At which point, in a completely ceremonial and mystical move, I elegantly upped it to 11 minutes. Eleven! Why? Because it felt magical and oddly satisfying. Like a little wink from the Universe saying, "Look at you, showing up."

Over time, the shifts were subtle but undeniable. I got less reactive. More curious. I didn't need to fix every feeling or chase every thought like a dog after a squirrel. And when I forgot to meditate for a day or two (or three), the fog came rolling in fast. Thicker. Stickier. With a generous side of annoyance and resentment. But here's the kicker: the solution is also faster now. Just tune in. Let go. The fog doesn't linger like it used to.

I've discovered that meditation is actually pretty easy—once I stopped obeying the imaginary rules I thought were required. I had this idea it was about sitting like a statue, clearing all thoughts, floating in a state of permanent bliss. Nope. Turns out, I still think. Constantly. I'm not here to be a monk. I'm here to be fully, wildly human.

One of the most freeing shifts came after listening to a very touching, moving, and inspiring meditation by the fabulous Sarah Blondin entitled ***"I Would Like to Give You Permission."*** I realized—holy shit—that was what had been missing. At some level, I had been unconsciously waiting for permission to *break the rules*. To just go with the flow. In meditation lingo, I didn't need to clear my thoughts. I only needed to watch them. I didn't have to shove them out of the room or chant them into submission. Just *watch*. And maybe even welcome them without inviting them to unpack. That little crack in the rules? It opened everything. Who fucking knew I was actually sitting inside myself this whole time, just... waiting. For permission. And now that I have it? I give myself permission for all sorts of things. All the time. It's delicious. Thank you Sarah!

So yes, I still think. I still get distracted. But now I know how to breathe. I know how to notice. I know how to sit with myself—not to fix, not to judge, just to *be*. And sometimes, in that space, the fog lifts just enough for a little love note to sneak in. Something simple. Something true.

And in that space—between the sigh and the smirk—something softens. Something opens. A little spark lights up the haze and says, "Hey you. Yes, you. You're not alone in there."

So yes, "I love YOU!" isn't so weird to say to myself after all. Especially when it's true. Especially when I can finally hear it.

When I Looked Up
When I looked up
and inward this day
there was graceful,
calm – *space*!

When I checked in
and checked out
my thoughts
some things were gone.

As if by magic
the tides had turned
from intrusive – busy
noisy – pushy – disturbing.

To stillness & serene
open space between
my ears – my feelings
my mouth & my actions.

This motionless – placid
clearing allows for
clarity – acceptance
awareness & breath.

The margin, the gap
provides, graciously,
unconditional
choices & freedom.

In the quiet
I can see my outline
I can begin to sense
my greatness & passion

waiting there, here inside

patiently, so bravely
unflappable & strong,
stoic, stolid, my rock.

Along my edges the
beauty creeps in
the joy, the hope,
a way to love.

Seeping in slowly
the space allows healing,
balance – even wisdom
to sneak in between the cracks.

And when I look up
from where I've been
hunched & crouching
I have *headroom*!

September 2021

Insanity
The sky-blue expecctations
klcy
The Hatred — red, bubbling, angry

WHERE THE LAVA LEADS

ON HATRED, HONESTY
AND LETTING GO

I recently completed a seven-day meditation course called ***OSHO - No Mind***. Each day consisted of one hour of "gibberish" followed by one hour of silent sitting. You can find more detailed explanations of these practices online, but here's the essence: the Gibberish is a cathartic release—a wild, uncensored outpouring of sounds and nonsense that dislodges stuck thought patterns and makes space for silence. At first, I felt silly and resistant. But by day three, the part of me that clung to "doing it right" began to dissolve. Something ancient and wordless started to rise.

That's when the river showed up.

One afternoon, just before the silent hour, the recorded voice of OSHO filled the ZOOM room. He said thoughts are like a muddy river full of debris, twigs, and swirling currents. Our job in meditation isn't to fix the river, clear it, or dive in with a strainer. The more you try to fix it, he said, the more you stir it up. Just watch! Meditation is just watching.

But what if the river you're watching isn't just muddy—it's boiling? What if it's not water at all, but lava—bubbling, angry, and scalding? I sat there, trying to be still, as this volcanic undercurrent surged through my chest and clenched my jaw. What the hell is *that*?

Judgment. That was the first word that surfaced. Followed closely by its darker twin: HATRED. This is where things got interesting. I don't see myself as hateful. Opinionated, sure. Irritated, often. But hatred? That felt taboo, extreme, like something I should be above. Even in my most critical moments, I would've called it disappointment, frustration, or moral concern. Hatred was a word reserved for villains. For racists and tyrants. For people in mobs, not people in meditation.

But sitting there, breath after breath, I felt it. The judgment that hides in my bones. The quick and slicing commentary I aim—first and fiercest—at myself. The disgust at my own imperfection. The resentment toward those who've hurt me. The tightness in my chest when I perceive hypocrisy, cruelty, or entitlement. And underneath it all, this dense, black tar. Sticky. Burning. Familiar.

There is no hatred without judgment. And judgment starts at home.

I've always spoken more freely about judgment than hatred. Judgment felt intellectual, something to explore or unpack in conversation. Hatred, on the other hand, felt like a radioactive word. Saying it out loud would make it real. But here's the thing: I've been navigating the river of my mind like a self-appointed cleanup crew. Tidying the banks. Organizing the flotsam. Pretending I'm just processing. But really? I've been trying to exile this exact force from my inner world—without ever letting it speak.

Hatred is messy. It makes us feel like bad people. Especially if you've been trying your whole life to be good.

In this meditation, I didn't scream or cry or punch pillows. I just sat and watched the lava roll. I let it burn. I let it tell me things I didn't want to know. That I still carry resentment. That some of my boundaries were built not from self-love, but from spite. That I've used spiritual concepts to mask contempt. That I've judged the judgers while secretly judging myself ten times harder.

And still, there was nothing to fix.

That's the part that cracked me open. OSHO's voice echoed: *Just watch.* My task was not to rationalize or reframe, not to hunt for silver linings or write affirmations. My only job was to witness the river, the lava, the hatred—and to keep sitting.

This wasn't about self-improvement. It was about honesty.

The silence that followed wasn't calm or sweet. It was sobering. It was real. It felt like meeting myself without makeup, mirrors, or apologies. It felt like standing in a dark cave with no torch, no exit, just the raw walls of my own psyche. But eventually, the cave breathed back. The hatred didn't swallow me. It softened. Not because I conquered it, but because I stayed.

Hatred can't survive in the light of awareness. It's not that it disappears—it transmutes. It reveals its roots. Most of mine? Old pain. Betrayal. Disappointment. Grief I hadn't let move through.

Anger I wasn't allowed to express. It was never about hating others. It was about parts of me I didn't know how to love.

So I made a little vow—not to be hatred-free, but to be hatred-aware. To notice the curl of contempt before it curdles into rage. To let the lava move, not freeze into armor. To soften the walls that judgment built. And to stop pretending I'm too evolved to feel what I feel.

Because the truth is, hatred exists. It lives in every culture, every system, every family. Naming it doesn't make it stronger. Naming it allows it to breathe. And maybe, eventually, to dissolve.

I left that meditation course with more clarity, not less. I didn't float out on a bliss cloud. I walked out with muddy feet, tear-streaked cheeks, and a strange kind of gratitude. Grateful for the honesty. Grateful for the fire. Grateful that, beneath it all, the river is still flowing.

And now, I watch.

Anger
See the flames of hell
Spit sparks that instantly ignite
Embers long smoldering
Deep inside the heart.
Don't quench the fire
Let it burn, baby.
Let it burn.
It lies smoking
But once lit brings
Insanity to pulse
Through the body
And the mind.
Explodes in an
Agonizing fury
Of rebellious thought
Incapable of holding still.
Frozen yet burning.
How to let it out
Without hurting someone,

Especially self?

From generations past
To present friends
Wounding without thought
Stabbing without awareness
Remember to burn
Baby, let it burn.
Outside – not in.
Dismembering your reality
The problem is then focused
Clear – Cold…
Unchanged it tries
To hide itself or
Become a camouflaged
Part of self.
Why is it, I'm mad?
Problems – no answers.
Where or upon what
Should I release my beast?
Anger is energy
The beast a natural being.
Nature can absorb,
It understands the beast within
Shout & scream
Release the soul
Release the cells of the poison
Anger
To us Poison
To her lover
Let it fly –
Let it burn, baby
Let it burn.

-July 1995

I SEE YOU

BEYOND THE BUBBLE

BUBBLE POPPED.
GRACE REVEALED.

I'm blushing with joy that the poems are flowing again. This is the way of it. I've learned that anxious desire or wistful wishing doesn't bring the words. The flow of wisdom is always present—I'm just not always tuned in. And that, too, is perfectly perfect.

But when I do tune in—when I hear the words, see the images, feel the cadence of something waiting to be spoken—I recognize it instantly. It's a gift, a pulse, a whisper, a flood.

I didn't grow up on Rumi or Mary Oliver. My gateway poetry drug was a dusty old book called ***Treasured Volume - An Anthology of Poems Collected by John Scott, 1967***—a gift my mother received from an old boyfriend. It somehow, thankfully, found it's way to my hands. These poems didn't float off into the mystical unknown—they rhymed, they made sense, they offered real-world wisdom in tidy little stanzas. Like my parents' vinyl collection was my access to music, this book was my backdoor into poetry: old-school, grounded, and sneakily profound. That's where the admiration started—and eventually, the writing.

So if poetry isn't usually your thing, I get it. But just for now, drop the eye-roll and let go of whatever ideas you're holding about what poetry *should* be. Read it aloud—softly, boldly, or dramatically, like you're auditioning for a part in a cosmic play. Shout it. Sing it. Let it move through you. And notice, if you will, whether something stirs. Your own wise self may just be listening.

A poem is just a pointer to something grand and lovely.

What it points to for you is yours alone. Enjoy.

Held & Free
In and out, round and round--
expanding, contracting,
tight—loose—tie it off.

Open wide, breathe it in.
Shut down, spit it out.
The sphere
of my experience
pulsates, glitters,
skims chaos,
tightens down--
lovely, cozy,
healing, quiet.

It is a sphere, isn't it?
Not a circle.
The energy ebbs and flows
in at least three dimensions,
probably nine—
in front, behind,
above, below,
left, right,
past, future,
now.

Some say, "Create a bubble"
to protect yourself--
against… what?
What you don't want?
I say, shift your perception,
pop the bubble.
Notice—your sphere was always there,
"protecting" you--
if you need protecting at all.

I'm not a fan of protection--
let nature take its course,
trust your knowing.
My sphere tightens,
taking stock, energy
ricocheting through the corridors

of memory, dream, and desire,
brushing past fear,
weaving through expectation.

I'll take my time inside.
No rush.
Enjoy your chaos, your drama--
I am here, drawn to my light,
curious about its paradox--
shutting down to open up,
withdrawing to advance,
pausing—listening--
to surrender, to love,
whatever comes next.

The soundest truth,
the one I choose to believe,
rises, spills--
pouring from the inside out.
Hello, my Love.
What's next?

- March 2025

October
LOVE
RESPONSIBILITY

LOCK & KEY

As the days fly by and the seasons shift from summer to winter, I find myself suspended in the beauty of autumn—wrapped in its light, colors, and warm, wispy breezes. Yesterday was a particularly perfect fall day. Autumn, with its fleeting nature, feels like a mirror to the shifts within me—vibrant and beautiful, yet temporary, a reminder that change is inevitable. The golden hues, the crisp morning air, and the falling leaves seem to whisper the importance of release, of letting go.

In this transition, I'm working to be graceful and patient with my own underlying transformation. Milestones approach and pass, and I observe them ahead, adjust and watch them gently pass into my rearview mirror. I am simply along for the ride. Lately, I've been in a holding pattern, implementing a major change in how I move through the world. During a recent meditation session, I received a clear, dispassionate message. Its simplicity and insight were unexpected, even miraculous. When the message arrived, it was as though a curtain had been pulled back. The audacity stunned me— I would never have thought of it on my own in a million years, and yet it resonated in a way that felt undeniable. It's strange how the simplest twists on perception or the awareness of a plucky fearless objective has the power to upend everything you thought you knew.

Communicating these changes to the people in my life has been a challenge—remaining mindful, honest, and present through it all. I'm learning to let go of my fears and expectations, navigating the delicate balance of sharing just enough with some, while pouring my heart out to others. By observing these conversations—my motives, feelings, and the eventual outcomes—I've grown a deeper appreciation for myself. My inner strength, my relationships, and, above all, my sense of love and responsibility toward myself and those closest to me have come into sharper focus. (When the coast is clear and all parties are informed with kindness and integrity I will share the details of this particular taboo evolution.)

Recently, the image of a lock and key surfaced during meditation, symbolizing my habits and aversions. I've avoided responsibility, and I've shied away from love, especially when it comes to myself. Responsibility and love—two concepts that I've long kept separate in my mind. I've treated responsibility like a burden, a task to be completed, while love was something elusive, often conditional. But now, I see how they intertwine. If love is the key to unlocking responsibility, then perhaps responsibility is the lock that safeguards true, deep self-love. One cannot exist without the other. There's a profound, until now unexplored, relationship between them. These concepts are the opposites of my current habits—hatred and avoidance.

David Hawkins, in his book, ***Letting Go: The Pathway of Surrender***, suggests that we open ourselves to the opposite of those lower frequency emotions. It's a slow, steady process: noticing the fear, avoidance, or discomfort. Name it and it's opposite then allowing ourselves to release the resistance. There is no specific action—just letting go of the resistance to the OPPOSITE. I feel hatred and avoidance, the opposite is love and responsibility. The intention is to release my resistance to love and responsibility! It's so simple, so easy! It all lies in observing, in noticing, and detaching. Letting go is not a one-time decision, but an ongoing practice. At first, it felt odd and too easy. But over time, I'm noticing that it is growing slowly, steadily like a good seed planted in ready soil. I just get to be patient and willing. No surprise there!

It's incredible what the mind can stir up, isn't it? Avoidance has shown up in subtle ways throughout my life—putting off important conversations, neglecting my own needs, pretending certain emotions don't exist or numbing them completely. I've often convinced myself that by avoiding something, I was maintaining peace, but now I see how it only creates inner turmoil. Slowly, I'm learning to sit with discomfort instead of running from it. And then there's responsibility. Of course, I've avoided taking care of my physical body. It was never taught to me as a priority, something one must do. I imagine that other children were taught how to exercise and maintain that body-mind-spirit balance. Right? I missed out. Poor me! Too late now... right?

No, it's not too late. And no, not "poor me." I've learned so many valuable things that brought me to where I am now, and I'm grateful for every last bit. Now, I get the chance to hone in on areas of my behavior, thoughts, and judgments that might cause greater problems down the line. It's never too late. The timing is, as always, precisely perfect. I have the time, the means, and the motivation, and I've realized it's something I must do for myself. In the past, partners may have "inspired" me to exercise, but that was vanity or people-pleasing. The source of the behavior matters—the motivation and intention mean everything. Now, my motive is love, and my timeframe is open, flexible, in tune with the Universe.

Coincidentally (or not), I'm starting another OSHO course today, also for 7 days. Can you guess the topic of this one? This new OSHO course feels like the perfect next step in my journey. I'm approaching it with a sense of curiosity and openness, eager to see what new insights will emerge. The topic, though I haven't fully revealed it yet, aligns perfectly with the questions I've been sitting with—themes of love, responsibility, and self-awareness. Stay tuned!

Blessed is the Source

Blessed is the Source of Bliss
Who offers me a path to Bliss.
May this be a day for setting aside expectations
and surrendering to the simple Truth of What Is
That I may remember and find
my way to what may be.

Blessed is the Source of Wisdom,
Who offers me a path to Wisdom.
May this be a day for heeding the
intuitive voice that whispers within.
May I be Open and Trusting,
With DELIGHT in life and the ONE who manifests it.

Blessed is the Source of Stillness,
Who offers me a path to Stillness.
May this be a day for patient belonging
and connection to the Reality of what is.
Observance and pausing to listen for grace and guidance.

Blessed is the Source of Kindness,
Who offers me a path to Kindness.
May this be a day for spacious mind
and fierce loving kindness toward all.

Blessed is the Source of Power,
Who offers me a path to Power.
May this be a day to shine
with the confidence and freedom,
Of No Desire and fearless being.

Blessed is the Source of Creativity,
Who offers me a path to Creativity.
May this be a day for acknowledging
and expressing my unique, never-recurring potentialities.
I am willing and give myself permission t
o be fully me in each moment.

Blessed is the Source of Moments,
Who offers me a path to Moments.
May this be a day for awareness and
presence in the moment.
Letting go and allowing the past to be past and
the present to be undiscovered and unbounded.

Blessed is the Source of Curiosity,
Who offers me a path to Curiosity.
May this be a day for exploring with Wonder
each and every thought, impulse, desire, emotion
and experience with the eyes of attention,
awe and inquiry.

Blessed is the Source of Forgiveness.
Who offers me a path to Forgiveness.
May this be a day for letting go and
being vulnerable to uncertainty.
May I be free of attachment to all past wounds,
hurts and take responsibility for the lessons they offer.

Blessed is the Source of Gratitude
Who offers me a path to Gratitude.
May this be a day for recognizing the gifts
pre-sent and the endless abundance of all things.
"I send you only angels."

Original Idea and some stanzas from Rabbi Shapiro's book ***The Sacred Art of Lovingkindness*** (page 47). OMG a MUST read!!! *Some modifications and additional original stanzas by Laurie Anne McCauley December 2021*

PULSE AND PAGES, PART 1

MUSCLE MEMORY, CELLULAR MYTHS, AND MY NEW VOICE

The image of a book was clear during meditation recently. The body is a book of stories waiting to be held, waiting to be explored and recreated, expunged, and reimagined. It holds the histories of lifetimes within its cells, chapters of laughter and grief, memories stored in muscle and bone, and sensations woven through veins like trails and pathways to adventures long ago. For the body, change just is—it is constant and flowing, unending. There is no need to be static; it is not possible to be static on this plane. The pages shift, always in motion, and I am here, reading them. I am listening. I am taking responsibility, practicing patience and kindness, learning to let go.

This new routine is like watching water boil—my mind can't resist checking the clock, adjusting the flame, shifting the pan, waiting for those first bubbles to form. I hover, overthinking every sensation, trying to make it happen faster. But of course, the more I try to control it, the longer it seems to take. Sometimes the body's stories need slow simmering, and maybe all I'm supposed to do is sit back, breathe, and let them unfold in their own time.

I do feel the progress; it ripples through me, gentle but undeniable. I can sense the difference intuitively, in my heart of hearts. A guided meditation suggests I listen to my own heartbeat. I struggle to find the pulse at my wrist, but it is still there, reassuring and human. I can't begin to comprehend it, but at least I know the forgotten language exists. My pulse is felt and fathomed more deeply, each beat more meaningful, more puzzling, like a language spoken only in quiet moments. My heart has become my storyteller, guiding me toward a kind of foreign, distant wisdom that has no need for words.

Can you imagine that you are created with one machine, designed solely to experience all this physical plane has to offer? This one mechanism, this one precious unit, is our sole instrument for touching the world. It is guided and linked to something beyond the physical, hovering here yet locked in time, willing and resistant all at once, both knowing and forgetting, remembering and learning. And we are to hold this instrument, this vehicle, with reverence. For any explanation or story we create to describe it feels inadequate, period.

As I meditated, I began with a bit of grumpiness—accusatory thoughts, doubts, negativity. They're familiar visitors. I am, since my last set of meditation classes, moving forward on my own with a blush of an idea on how to rewrite my own body's stories. Yet impatience remains a close friend of mine… we're tight! I'm making new friends with love, patience, responsibility, and power. It's uncomfortable and strangely magnetic. That old saying, "Make new friends but keep the old" does not apply here! I am looking forward to letting go of my very good, very old friends: fear, avoidance, resistance, blame, and impatience.

I imagine these old companions slowly receding, but not like a wave on the sand—that's much too quick. No, perhaps more like a season passing, but even that moves too fast for this process. We move from summer to fall to winter in only weeks, and this change feels far slower. So what analogy can I use? Perhaps it's like moving from childhood to puberty or fertility to barrenness; the shifts in the human body take years, lifetimes even. I'm beginning to appreciate the depth of these changes, realizing that generations of genetics and evolution bear upon this body in my lifetime. This journey, my body's story, is shaped by the ages. I recall a passage from Eckhart Tolle in **Stillness Speaks**: battling and fighting aren't effective since there is no enemy. It's not about "doing" anything, only remaining alert and aware. Notice the thoughts and consider the source.

For now, in this moment, I get to exercise my creativity and keep my mind engaged as I journey toward alignment with my body-mind. I so enjoyed my recent trip north, when the original plans fell through, the sudden freedom from a time commitment was invigorating, like the spontaneous rush of clear air. I got to jump into the flow of life without a project, destination, or appointment! I remembered in Julia Cameron's, **The Artist's Way**, advice about scheduling a weekly artist's date. I've read and worked through the entire book alone and with several friends over the decades since I found the book in the 1990's. From what I recall, the Artist Date is a once-weekly, festive, solo expedition to explore something that interests you. The Artist Date need not be overtly "artistic"– think mischief more than mastery. Artist Dates fire up the imagination. They spark whimsy. They encourage play.

I checked the movies playing at the local theater. I watched a few trailers, curious if something might feel entertaining, enlightening, or informative. I considered adding a trip to the cinema as one adventure on a weekly date. Movies, however, won't be making my solo adventure list—at least not the ones on the marquee right now. It was instantly apparent, just watching the trailers, that this is precisely where a lot of my delusional expectations about relationships came from! Instead, I want to keep my mind and emotions open to my own creative endeavors rather than immersing myself in someone else's story. As moving or poignant as their tales of love, fulfillment, loss, or drama may be, thanks to meditation, clarity, and a better relationship with the present moment, I choose, for now, to listen with patience and kindness to my own heart's song. I'll tune into my own radio station, catching up on my own reactions, preferences, loves, dislikes, and curiosities.

Over and out.

There is
NO WAY
"one" "WAY"

PULSE AND PAGES, PART 2

WHEN LISTENING BECOMES LIVING

The image of the body as a living book (Pulse and Pages 11/2024) has stayed with me. Not just a book to be read, but one to be rewritten, revisited, and reimagined over time. This body, this mechanism, remains a constant storyteller — shifting, flowing, revising. The stories haven't stopped unfolding; they have only deepened.

Since that first vision months ago, I find myself in a new phase of listening. Some chapters feel familiar — pages I've skimmed before but now have the patience to read more carefully. Other chapters seem to have appeared from nowhere, surprising me with their complexity, tenderness, and weight.

My mantras still hold true — *There is nothing to fear. There is nothing to prove. There is nothing to fix. There is nothing wrong. There is nothing missing.* But now they feel less like something I'm reciting and more like a natural hum beneath my days, shaping the way I meet myself. I don't have to work so hard to remember them. They are starting to *remember me.*

Meditation is no longer a morning chore, no longer a battle to overcome habitual grumpiness. Something has shifted — perhaps the release of so many trapped emotions has finally cleared a wider channel. Whatever the cause, the background noise in my mind has softened into a kind of calm grace. Where there was once defending, resisting, and protecting, there is now a steady, quiet openness.

And seriously, this is *huge.* I notice it in all kinds of small moments: standing in line, sitting across from a friend, driving alone. I can pull back what feels like a thin veil — a veil of watchfulness, anxiousness — and simply listen, open-hearted and unguarded.

It reminds me of standing inside a greenhouse in winter. At first, everything seems cold, brittle, and silent. But if you stand still long enough, you realize it's full of life: the small creak of growing branches, the almost inaudible hum of energy rising. That's how this new listening feels — like stepping into a living space that doesn't need my defense, my opinions, or my point of view to survive. I don't have to perform. I don't have to prove anything. I can just be there, breathing.

Life, of course, hasn't stayed still either. In recent weeks, I've discovered the Landis Arboretum, a beautiful place for walking, wandering, and scheduling Artist's Dates with myself. The idea of solo adventures, once so tentative, now feels natural and nourishing. My calendar has also filled up, gently and serendipitously, with new dates: old acquaintances who have appeared seemingly out of nowhere, offering renewed friendship, conversation, and laughter at just the right time. And then there's California. A trip I decided on with almost no overthinking — an instinctive yes. Jo, a friend from Australia, is leading a seminar there, and it felt easier, lighter, more fun to fly across the country than to wonder endlessly whether or not I should go. Will I simply observe? Will I jump in and participate? I don't know yet. But it doesn't matter. Any adventure is a lovely adventure. The spirit of exploration itself feels like the right answer.

I came across a Rumi poem this morning that I hadn't heard before. His words have been shadowing me too — especially a few stanzas from "The Community of Spirit" that seem to capture everything I'm learning, everything I'm living right now:

> *Close both eyes*
> *to see with the other eye.*
>
> *Open your hands,*
> *if you want to be held.*
>
> *Sit down in this circle.*
> *Be empty of worrying.*
> *Think of who created thought!*
>
> *Why do you stay in prison*

I'm beginning to enjoy the mystery again. Not because I solved it, but because I finally stopped trying to manage it. This is what space creation was always about — not a performance, not a purge, but an invitation. And now, with so much static cleared, I can feel the payoff: a naturally calm background where the goodness just flows, no longer blocked, no longer tangled. I didn't force it. I just made room. And something wise and kind rushed in to fill the space.

There is nothing to fear. There is nothing to prove. There is nothing to fix. There is nothing wrong.

There is nothing missing. Honestly, it feels like switching from dial-up internet to fiber optic soul-speed. Static quieter. Drama more distant. Subscription to chaos: *unsubscribed.* Thank you, Spirit. Thank you, nervous system. Thank you, stubborn human heart. May it stay quiet and glorious for a good long while. (And just in case I forget again, maybe let Spirit stash the map somewhere safe —far from my usual hiding spots - until I ask nicely.) Over and out — and tuned in.

Pivot
Esther
4·25·22

SPUN OUT, SOAKED & SAVED

MEAN PEOPLE HAPPEN. PIVOT ACCORDINGLY.

I'm practicing paying attention to my emotions and feelings. Well, neighbor, let me tell you — I went on *quite* a ride today! They grabbed me by the heels, held me upside down, and shook HARD. Fuck!

The physical adrenaline rush alone was enough to keep me zooming for days. My instinctual, habitual, fear-and-people-pleasing-fixing brain pathways were LIT UP. I mentioned a few days ago how I'd serendipitously reconnected with some old friends and acquaintances, and I was looking forward to blossoming renewed connections and sharing and — holy fucking shit — so much for *those* delusional expectations! I can say more clearly now: I have opportunities galore to practice my new skills... with some old fart friends.

This morning, I received a text message informing me that being friends with me would "compromise their values." Strange doesn't even begin to cover it. I started tracking the feelings as they arrived: first up, adrenaline — with no particular direction to the energy, just ZING. Next came defensiveness and explaining — a flashing impulse to set the record straight. I was obviously and egregiously misunderstood, right? OF COURSE the best, most normal thing would be to correct the error! Immediately! Vigorously! Off I'd go, building an argument, constructing examples, spinning up explanations like a maniacal cotton candy machine. Surely, surely I was the victim here. Surely!

Along with defensiveness came a big fat serving of "being right" and "looking good." How could she think that of me? She didn't even talk to me about it! Cue the old familiar soundtrack: wronged, misunderstood, mistreated, unfair, blah blah blah. SPINNING. I took more than a few deep breaths. I managed — miracle of miracles — to stay standing as the observer, not the participant. I allowed. I accepted. I talked calm and peace to myself. I let the justifiable rage and righteous upset float on by. There I sat — on the riverbank, smiling gently — when grief came roaring in next.

Tears. Sadness. Ached-out heart. Sadness for the state of affairs: that people can be so attached to their own beliefs. That connections can close so fast. That intimacy and friendship can turn to dust with no conversation. But I didn't let the "Why? Why? Why?" machine fire up too hard. Deep breath. Tears. Another deep breath. Another wave passed.

And then — finally — gratitude. Gratitude that the would-be friend at least recognized their discomfort and acted with integrity. (Or, you know, acted in some way.) I'm guessing it wasn't an easy message to send. At least I hope not. Gratitude for the clarity. Gratitude for the closure. Gratitude for the truth that hurt but freed.

Then, forgiveness. For her. For me. For the pain-bodies and trapped emotions that collide all day long in all of us, just trying to do our best. I'm noticing echoes now — echoes of the first flood of feelings: defending, people-pleasing, fixing, justifying, explaining, spinning wild reasons and scenarios in my head to prove (to whom?) that I am right, wise, good, fair, better, smarter...

STOP. Practice. Practice. Practice. Out of the floodwaters. Back to the shore.

What a fucking amazing experience. Thank you, old friend (past tense). You gave me a smashing, smashing gift. Out of the water, onto the shore — over and over — until the message finally tattoos itself into my neurons: No need to dive down that dark alley. No need for the spinning. No need for external validation to know my own worth. I am also exceedingly grateful — and here, I 1000% concur with ***David Sedaris' Master Class*** — WHAT DO PEOPLE DO WHO CAN'T WRITE ABOUT THIS SHIT??? Thank you, Spirit, for giving me the glorious outlet of writing.

No need for more wondering, questioning, analyzing, or proving. Just standing here, letting the waves break... and roll on down the river. Grateful. Forgiving. Free.

Witness
I am witness
to the young pecker
the monarch
the breeze
the cloudy sun sky

I am witness
to the weeds
and peppers
buttons and poppies
the warmth
and the chill

I am witness
to a numb butt cheek
hopeful noisy
RC car
The OM in my ear
and my purpel pen

I am witness
to my slight smile
(at misspelling purple)
and deep breath
and the smell
of espresso – just there
in the cup with patina

I am witness
to all this at once
and singly
the man I love
pulling weeds
bent over
blackbird migration
on his tongue

I am witness
this moment
all and enough
for me as I sit
in my clearing
as I wait
hands spread open
cupped

I am witness
while I wait
my life goes before me
in and out
back and forth
memories and
magical visions
mix and flow
nicely – lovely

I witness my own
attachment – kindness
anger – joy – fear
what?
mysteries and
mythical emotions
like puffy clouds
wander and scatter
across my horizon
dark – light
thunder – rain

I witness my birth
my passions
my death and
stillness sublime

delicious
lovingkindess
I am witness.

- July 2021

PART FIVE
LANDMARKS &
TRAIL MARKERS
RECOGNIZING PROGRESS & MILESTONES

Tiny clicks, sudden vistas, wobbly ground, unexpected excitement, and the urge to share your journey.

These are the moments you remember—the unexpected forks in the trail, the stacked-stone cairns (those little rock towers left like breadcrumbs), the graffiti on the trees. The gut punches and glitter bombs of realization that yell: *Hey! Pay attention—this matters.* This section holds the thresholds and turning points—the flashes of insight, emotional mile markers, and those suspiciously well-timed synchronicities that make you stop mid-step. These aren't textbook teachings—they're field notes. Real-life rambles, aha!s, and accidental discoveries that left a dent. They may not shout, but they stick. You might trip over one in your own life too—if you're paying attention. So pause here. Make a mark on your map. This is where something shifted. And just in case no one's said it lately: You are here. And it matters.

Surrender
Listen

THE WRIST REMINDER

INKED IN. SHARPIE-TESTED. SPIRIT APPROVED.

I had the word *Surrender* tattooed on my left wrist in 2014—a milestone moment, etched in ink. For months and months I tested the word and the place with a Sharpie. I wanted to be sure that it would be a message for all times of life, something that would resonate and hold true no matter my position in the ever-changing world. It wasn't just a design choice—it was a decision to honor what I knew would continue to unfold. Something that would still matter decades from now. It does. (And yes, I tested it in Sharpie first. For months. That's just how I roll.)

Indeed, it has proved to be a very valuable and ongoing message that resonates. Apparently, I have spent my entire life, possibly since my first breath when I got whacked, until now, resisting. Resisting people, places, things, nature, life, my good ideas, my creative ideas, my bad ideas, numbing out, avoiding and resisting... my top three unhealthy priorities.

Anything that has taken on such a vital part of my programming is bound to take time to release and reprogram. I encountered a whole new and curious level of resistance when it comes to day-to-day operations, people, and behaviors. It's easiest to explain in terms of expectations and disappointment; passion and apathy.

I expect people to be awake and kind; I'm constantly disappointed by what I perceive as humans acting stupid and mean or aware and malicious... This sense of justice and injustice in the world at large has caused me angst and frustration, resentment and suffering... I HAVE allowed my resistance to human nature as it is, reality, to get to me and make me angry, anxious, and hopeless. I take full responsibility for this dis-service to myself. I didn't know what I didn't know.

Now that it's clear that Reality just IS and it's not my fault or my job to fix it... holy cow, what a relief! The ripples and waves of relief keep coming on shore and washing over me, again and again! How lovely! This surrender is not defeat. It's oxygen. It's softness. It's room to move, breathe, and respond differently. I didn't know how much tension I was holding until I started to let go.

My natural healing and wholeness progresses as I come to peace with nature, with humans, with Reality. This is the way for me to explore my relationship with myself, with food, and with exercise and self-care. No other path will provide long-term, meaningful unity and peace. And when this particular journey is concluded, I look forward to the next challenge. And so I stare at the word on my wrist and marvel at the wonders revealed in such a simple word and the wisdom that showed up when I chose it as a lifelong reminder.

One I accepted without knowing the full journey it would take me on. I'm so glad I said yes. And next time I test a milestone in Sharpie? I'll know to pay attention—it's probably sacred. Honestly, this tattoo joins a growing collection of body-based wisdom. It lives in good company alongside *Listen With a Pretty Heart* and, of course, *Paws to Wonder.* That last one always makes me smile—because sometimes it really does just take a pause. Or a paw. Or both. To remember that presence is power, curiosity is holy, and wonder never fails.

Turns out, my tattoos aren't declarations. They're invitations. They whisper when I forget, nudge when I stall, and remind me that wisdom isn't something I find—it's something I'm learning to live. Inked in, yes. But also unfolding, pulse by pulse, moment by moment. One word at a time.

(And for anyone feeling squeamish about tattoos—no worries. You can stick with a Sharpie and keep your epidermis tattoo needle free. I did for months. But some reminders are just too good not to make permanent.)

Heart's Song

There's a new scent in the air.
Odd… yet enticing.
It comes in waves,
Yet lingers, inviting.

Out with the old
In with the new.
Explore a new way
Today's a new day.

Yesterday's gone
But not forgotten.
It lingers on
Till all's forgiven.

Moving forward
But dragging
Habit's past
Cannot last.

Nose to the wind,
Let the scent
Lead on
Till the past is gone.

So much at stake.
Work it out,
Ask the trees
Talk to the lake.

Pay attention.
Dive and fly.
Swallow fear,
A birth is near.

Go to where
You've dreamed.
The place you belong
Listen to heart's song.

- 2001

THE MELTDOWN WAS THE MIRACLE

MOMENTS OF WONDER.
HOLIDAY EDITION

The holiday season has a way of amplifying everything. Twinkling lights, the warmth of tradition, the expectations, the subtle grief, the forced cheer. It's not just the gifts and gatherings—it's the emotional stew of memory, obligation, and hope. For anyone on a path of personal growth, the holidays aren't just festive—they're a final exam. They stir up attachments, awaken old roles, and offer more spiritual "practice opportunities" than any silent retreat.

That's why this year, as I tried to stay rooted in new perspectives and rhythms, every little moment became a kind of checkpoint. How am I doing *now*? Can I stay curious here? Can I stay open *here*? Magic, I've realized, isn't just the sparkling part of the season. It's also what shows up in those small, tension-soaked moments that crack us open.

Magic, for me, has been showing up in the smallest details—a slant of morning light, the steam rising from a cup of tea, the sound of footsteps down a hallway where I'm just a guest. It's not in grand epiphanies—it's in how I respond when something unexpected derails my carefully managed plan. Like, say, losing my phone at my mother-in-law's.

I didn't even notice until hours later. I was home, finally in stretchy pants, thinking I'd earned my solo wind-down time. Then came the realization: my phone was gone. Cue the spiral. Was it lost? Left behind? Stolen? Did I leave it in the guest room or on the kitchen counter in the middle of all that noise and casserole coordination? My brain jumped to conclusions and then backflipped into panic.

The timing could not have been more inconvenient—or more

perfect. In the pressure-cooked environment of a family holiday gathering, surrounded by subtle judgments and miscommunications and the sound of someone else loading a dishwasher wrong, it was as if the universe yanked away my last connection to comfort and control.

At first, I panicked. My mind spun worst-case scenarios involving data theft, missed messages, a cascade of imagined consequences. I paced, grumbled, and tried to do that thing where you pretend not to care while you very much care. My hands felt empty, and I felt twelve years old and unmoored. But once the initial wave passed, something curious happened. I had the rare chance to observe my own reaction unfold in real-time. And behind the fear was something else: trust.

I got to feel it all. The worry, the helplessness, the grief of disconnection. And then, a shift. I remembered the practice. I remembered I didn't have to spin. I let it settle. I breathed. I accepted. I even laughed. And suddenly, the whole situation transformed into an unexpected gift. A chance to practice patience. To surrender. To observe the tight little loops my nervous system still runs when things don't go to plan. And that—that awareness—felt like a milestone.

Earlier that morning, before the gathering, I had made tea. The sun was just coming up, and the steam rose in lazy spirals from my cup. Bits of spice and moisture lifted like dancers, moved by the soft breath of the house and the warm push of furnace air. I paused to notice it—the way the light caught the vapor, the swirl of cinnamon or clove or something sweet. For a moment, I was aware of everything: the scent, the warmth, the quiet thrill of being alive inside that ordinary scene.

Even if I knew the science behind it—how heat lifts particles, how air circulates—there would still be magic in it. Because behind all the explanations, the deeper truth remains: something unseen is always at work. The Mover. The force behind the forces. Present and playful. Wise and winking. Always offering invitations. Sometimes through joy. Sometimes through mild holiday chaos.

What if every experience—even the inconvenient or uncomfortable ones—held that same potential for magic? Not magic with wands and chants and glittering potions, but the kind that happens when you *see*. When you soften. When you stay curious.

I think we're all born with the ability to see the extraordinary, but we forget. We get efficient. Distracted. Logical. We stop asking where the wonder went, and start accepting numbness as normal. But it's still there. The world is still enchanted. We just have to shift the lens.

The enchanted world isn't fiction—it's frequency. It hums underneath everything. I've come to believe that curiosity, creativity, and compassion are the secret keys. They're not personality traits; they're portals. They open me back up to the thrill of simply being alive.

And this path isn't about floating above real life or bypassing the messy parts. This is about walking straight into the mess with eyes wide open, ready to witness what unfolds. Even in the hard moments. Especially in the hard moments.

So yes—losing my phone at my mother-in-law's, surrounded by inherited patterns and forced small talk and the awkward shuffle of sleeping arrangements, became a genuine practice. A portal. A test. And also, weirdly, a celebration. Because I didn't spin as long this time. I didn't need to be rescued. I remembered that nothing was really missing. That I was okay. That the moment could be enough.

That's the real marker, isn't it? Not whether life feels perfect, but whether I remember how to come back to center when it doesn't. Whether I can find a little softness inside the storm. Whether I can make peace with what's happening without needing it to be different first.

As we step into the rest of the season—or the new year, or the next family gathering—I'm holding onto that. The memory of steam rising from tea. The echo of my own breath as I chose presence over panic. The quiet thrill of remembering that I get to choose what lens I use.

This is what the holiday season gave me: perspective. Practice. And a milestone moment, quietly disguised as a logistical inconvenience. And honestly, I'll take it. Because that's magic too.

Magic
The Magic
Stands up – Waving
"Heeere am I – Over heeere.

"I'm back,
though I never left.
I'm alive, and Well!

"Thanks for digging me up,
rooting me out,
Re-dis-covering all that I am.

"You are in for a treat,
a magnificent ride.
I'm Robert, today I'll be your guide.

("Just for today,
nothings forever, tomorrow
is Sal, or Joy or Max Clever.)

"So… you are just a tourist
a quick passer-thru
You won't feel at home
You're really not meant to.

"Keep it airy and light,
wander on don't alight
walk around slowly
Notice, observe every sight,

"Serious-ness is the fall
of it all – beware!
come along, stay awake
enjoy and be jolly.

"What's fun – so amusing
and true to the core
YOU set the stage and
YOU keep the score!"

- July 2020

WHACK
illing
ores
log
h'n
ALM
ind
Peon

OUTLOOK VS. OUTCOME
THE MARKER I ALMOST MISSED

I first heard it during my *Meditation Teacher Training* with davidji. A tiny phrase that grabbed me so hard I had to pause the session and write it down: *"We have control over our outlook, but never the outcome."* That's it. Simple. Brilliant. Exactly what I needed to remember.

He says a lot of things that land—questions like, "Who am I? What am I grateful for? Am I willing to be the best version of myself today?"—but that line was the one that tattooed itself across my morning. We get to plant the intention, but we don't get to force the harvest. We can ask, hope, imagine, envision. And then we let go. We give it to the Universe "to handle."

This has become a micro-practice for me. I'll whisper an intention—clarity, peace, connection—and immediately follow it with: "And now I give this to the Universe to handle." It keeps me honest. Keeps me out of fantasy outcomes. Keeps me from playing cosmic event planner.

It also reminds me of what I'm actually here for. I'm not the Director of Results. I'm not on the Outcomes Committee. But I am responsible for what I bring, how I show up, what energy I offer. My job is the *outlook*, not the scoreboard.

Still, I sometimes forget. When I care deeply. When I've worked hard. When I want to believe good behavior guarantees good results. But as someone once reminded me: "The world doesn't run on fairness. It runs on physics, friction, and other people's free will." (I wish that had been me. I'd put it on a mug.)

Here's the truth: I've spent too much of my life trying to guarantee outcomes by fine-tuning my behavior. If I say the right thing, do the right thing, anticipate every scenario, then surely I'll get the desired result. Spoiler: that's not how any of this works. People still get mad. Plans still fall apart. And sometimes the opposite of what I hoped for ends up being the very thing I needed.

So I'm learning to unhook. Not detach in the cold, unfeeling way, but in the curious, soul-preserving way. I let go *with love*. I hold hope, not expectation. I tend my outlook like a garden—sunlight, water, compost, and space—and let the blooms surprise me.

The older I get, the more I realize this is the spiritual game: show up with integrity and joy, and trust that the ripples are handled. Maybe not always visible. Maybe not even in my lifetime. But still—handled.

And on days when the clouds of doubt or frustration roll in (because they do), I sit with them. I stop swatting at butterflies and bees. I breathe. I reread this poem I wrote on a very cloudy day, and remember that all of it—the bugs, the breeze, the brightness and blur—is part of the process.

Clouds and Butterflies

The fears hover like clouds,
always, floating, drifting
blocking the light
filtering all that I experience

The bees & butterflies, my expectations,
fuss and flit and buzz about
distracting my attention
from the moment - the beauty
the truth, the unity that is reality.

There is nothing to be "done"
with the clouds or the bugs
They will not depart with all my wishing
no matter how much I pray or meditate
or practice or work or desire.

There is only to sit observing
in the clearing
calm and flowing.
Don't swat or hide or run.
Resistance is futile.

Only breathe & pause to wonder.
Notice don't think.
Observe don't judge.
Remember all is well and be grateful.

- April 2022

WORDS  for 2025

TRUST
Confident · Faith · Certainty · Reliance · Optimism · Acceptance
RESPONSIBLE · obligation · DUTY · Commitment
Rely on ENTRUST · Bet on · Confidence in · RESPONSIBILITY
CUSTODY - CARE - GUARDIANSHIP · Protection · observation
CONFIDENCE - Happiness — CALM - cheerful - Positive - SUNNY
Expectation · Belief · Anticipation · Assumption · Bank on
Innocence · naivete · SIMPLICITY · un-worldliness... ACCEPT

RESPONSIBLE
Dutiful · Respectful · Conscious · Intentional · Self-conscious -
♡ GROWN UP · Sensible · Mature · POWERFUL · TENDER
Reliable · Dependable · Trustworthy · Capable · Stable · TRUE · loyal
Passionate · Kind · Thoughtful · Fit · Intelligent · Clever · Bright
Accountable · At the Helm · BOUND TO · Bonded TO · Engaged in
CAUSATIVE · CAUSAL · Pivotal · Connecting · supportive

ACCEPT
- Receive · Bear · shoulder · take on · tackle · undertake
Admit · adopt · Believe · Understand · concede
CONSENT · AGREE · approve · SAY YES TO · WELCOME · Greet
ALLOW · EMBRACE · Agree · settle · decide · compromise
Believe TRUST RESPECT follow ACKNOWLEDGE · FAVOR · Esteem
Comply FOLLOW OBEY LISTEN observe · heed · Consider

ACCOUNTABLE
- RESPONSIBLE - OBLIGED
Expected - reasonable - understandable BOUND NATURAL
Justified · Logical FRANK - TRANSPARENT HONEST - IN CONTROL
Probable · Traceable · Detectable · Justified
OPEN Candid outspoken ASWERABLE · Actionable · Litigable - Suable ☺
WILLING truthful Reporting IN CONTROL
Subject · culpable · OBLIGED · obligated · Pliant
obediant AMENABLE - compliant - COOPERATIVE - submissive

COMMITMENT
an obligation that restricts freedom
RESPONSIBILITY · DUTY · Burden
Pledge · Promise · Vow · Decision · OATH · TRUSTWORTHY · DEPENDABLE
PASSION · Eagerness · enthusiasm
Persistance · Perserverance · Tenacity - Resolve - GRIT · Guts · VIGOR

TRUST - RESPONSIBILITY - DUTY - POWER - CONTROL
Obligation

INVESTMENT · dedication · sacrifice - SURRENDER
deprivation · service · Yielding

THE WAY OF WORDS

A WORD A YEAR KEEPS
THE FLOW GOING

At some point, I started choosing a word for the year—and not a cozy one. I mean a word that makes me a little uncomfortable, maybe even a little terrified. Like many of my best rituals, it showed up quietly, skipped the spiritual branding, and stuck around anyway.

One day I was jotting down mantras in a journal. Next thing I knew, I was crowd-sourcing synonyms like a scholar on a quest, whispering *this is the one* to a Post-it as if it were a sacred scroll. Some years the word arrives in a flash. Other years I chase it around like a cat with a laser pointer. One thing I've learned: the word is always on its own schedule.

Case in point—last year's word: *Freedom*. It didn't come gently. I had to sit with it. I had to talk myself into it. But then, over time (and not always comfortably), it landed. And let me tell you, it wasn't just the Instagram version of freedom—barefoot at the beach with a smoothie and no inbox. It was gritty. It meant letting go of roles I thought I had to play. It meant saying no when I was wired to say yes. It meant owning my time, my energy, and the narrative running in my head. Freedom showed up in my relationships, in my thoughts, in my schedule, and in more subtle crevices than I expected. It didn't always feel good. But it always felt true.

And here's the fun twist: now that it's 2025, *Freedom* is just starting to show off. It's like she got comfortable and now wants to hang out all the time. Some days I think I'm only just beginning to understand her. So while I'm over here trying to pick a *new* word, last year's word is still unpacking its bags and lighting incense. Honestly, I think she might have moved in.

That's the thing about this whole one-word practice: it rarely sticks to its calendar year. The impact runs on soul time. A word might whisper through for twelve months and then roar into relevance five years later. It's like planting a seed and realizing you accidentally signed up for a forest.

Still, despite (or maybe because of) that chaos, I keep doing it. Each December, I gather candidates. I use an app called Word Hippo (highly underrated name, by the way) to dig into the definitions, synonyms, antonyms, and strange cousins of whatever word has caught my eye. This year's list? A real party. I've got *Trust, Responsibility, Acceptance, Accountable,* and *Commitment* lined up like suspects in a spiritual lineup. All of them stir something uncomfortable in me. Which, let's be honest, is probably a sign they're onto something.

Trust feels like the one most likely to win—if only because it freaks me out the most. It dares me to let go of my white-knuckle grip on certainty. To surrender the analysis. To let life do its thing without my constant commentary. It sounds beautiful… in theory. In practice? Eek.

Responsibility wants me to grow up—kindly, yes, but still. It's the word that says, "Hey, you're the adult now. Maybe stop blaming Mercury retrograde and hydrate." It feels like radical self-respect in action. Also exhausting.

Acceptance is soft and deceptively fierce. It invites me to stop defending, stop fixing, stop performing. To sit down in the truth of what is and call it enough. It has a quiet power, like moss growing over a wound.

Accountable sounds like something my inner teenager wants to rebel against, but when I lean in, I realize it's not about punishment —it's about integrity. About choosing alignment on purpose. It's not "be better," it's "be honest."

And *Commitment?* Commitment is the one raising its hand in the back, waiting patiently to be noticed. It asks: can you keep showing up, even when the shine wears off? Can you follow through—not for perfection, but for the quiet joy of keeping your own word?

Honestly, they all feel like good choices. By which I mean: they all make me slightly nauseous. But I've learned to trust that nausea. If a word makes me a little squirmy, a little breathless, it's usually because it's pointing at some long-held fear I'm ready to outgrow. It's not a punishment. It's a portal.

210

Sometimes I'm tempted to choose a "safe" word. Something I already know how to do. Like *Curiosity*. Or *Joy*. Or just keep *Freedom* and call it good. But this year marks my 60th trip around the sun, and honestly? I'm ready for something bolder. Something that might require me to dig a little deeper, trust a little more, and step into territory I've been cleverly avoiding. Something that calls out the parts of me that are ready to be seen, heard, and lived.

Of course, none of this is linear. The word won't work on cue. It won't show its true face in January and then retire in December. It'll wiggle into conversations, dreams, arguments, cravings, and long walks. It'll test me, tease me, surprise me. And eventually, it'll change me. That's how it works. These words aren't just anchors or intentions. They're trail markers. Landmarks along the winding path of becoming.

So I'm holding the list loosely. I'm asking, not analyzing. I'm letting the word come when it's ready. Maybe it'll land while I'm journaling. Maybe while I'm washing dishes. Maybe it already has, and I just need to admit it. Either way, I trust the process—even if I don't fully understand it.

What about you? What word would you choose? Would you stick with something cozy and familiar—or pick the one that makes your stomach flip? Would you let yourself be led by something simple and sacred and a little wild?

It only takes one word to start. One word to shift your attention, shape your days, and open a new chapter.

Just don't expect it to follow the calendar.

Surrender
For your self
For your life

Stand strong
Surrender
Trust and
Let go forever.

For the love

Of your life
And the planet
We thrive on
Stand strong
Surrender
Trust and
Let go forever.

All you believed
Is empty
All you think
Delivered
Stand strong
Surrender
Trust and
Let go forever.

Love yourself
Truly
Every inch
Every "fault"
Stand strong
Surrender
Trust and
Let go forever.

Passion beckons
Fulfillment
Purpose calls
You forth
Stand strong
Surrender
Trust and
Let go forever.

Together we
Create tomorrow

Love holds the
Difference we make
Stand strong
Surrender
Trust and
Let go forever.

- June 2002

DISCOMFORT
AHEAD

THRESHOLD OF WILLINGNESS

NUMEROLOGY AND OTHER DISTRACTIONS

I've always loved numbers. Not in a full-on numerology way—though I've dabbled—but because they feel orderly. Clean. Patterned. My sober date is 04-14-14, and something about that symmetry just felt right. Back in 2022, when I sat down to write on 02-02-2022, I felt that same spark of potential. A moment worth paying attention to. It felt like an invitation, a doorway. But I was still trying to kick that door down instead of simply opening it.

That year, I thought the problem was food. Again. I'd just restarted *yet another* program, convinced this time would be different. I signed up, bought the streaming workouts, mapped out the meals, and even found joy in the novelty. But underneath the surface, something felt… off. Familiar, too familiar. Like I'd been here before. A hundred times. And every time I'd been shocked—*shocked!*—that it didn't work.

Einstein may have said the definition of insanity is doing the same thing over and over and expecting different results. I thought I understood that. But I didn't. Because I kept believing that *tweaking* the strategy—this new diet, that new tracker, a different kind of discipline—was something new. It wasn't. It was the same damn thing in a new wrapper. The core pattern hadn't changed at all.

What I see now, in hindsight, is that it was never really about the method. It was about *me* and my absolute unwillingness to be uncomfortable. Not pain. Not trauma. Just discomfort. Hunger. Soreness. Stillness. Emotional turbulence. The slightest twitch of craving or resistance, and I'd go straight into planning, fixing, managing, avoiding. I thought I had to control everything—every variable, every bite, every outcome—when really I just didn't want to *feel* the stretch. My glass ceiling wasn't made of discipline. It was made of avoidance.

For decades, I believed the lie that I had to make *every* change at once. When I tried to quit smoking and drinking simultaneously, I told myself it had to be a package deal or nothing. That delusion kept me stuck for years. It wasn't until alcohol dragged me down hard and fast that I surrendered to reality and prioritized the greater danger. That was the only way forward: not both, not perfect, just *one thing at a time.*

I see that same dynamic now in my health and movement patterns. Food, for the most part, is neutral now. I've done the work there. I've healed enough to be done with obsessive diets. But fitness —that one still stings. That one still beckons. And now, finally, I understand that it deserves its *own* season. Its own rhythm. Its own set of experiments, practice, play, and commitment. I can't overhaul my entire life in a single sweep. That was the old delusion. My DMGS (Divine Magical Guidance System) reminds me gently: *Which part is yours to tend this month?*

Looking back, that day—02-02-2022—was a beautiful number. A beautiful trap. I mistook the symmetry for certainty. A signal that something was about to click. But nothing clicks until I stop trying to *make* it work and start letting it *move* through me. Numbers won't save me. The next perfect system won't either. Only willingness will. Willingness to be uncomfortable. To be present with the discomfort long enough to let it transform.

It's taken me three more years to really admit this. And now, in 2025, I'm finally more curious about what I resist than what I crave. Resistance is the compass. That edge I didn't want to cross? That's the doorway. That's where the magic lives—not in the number, but in the willingness to follow the *right* next step, one sacred shift at a time.

Let Go
Scattered thoughts of life – love – change
Pleasantly strewn, with no attachment or fear.
Just thoughts wandering in and out,
Wondering at life and it's purpose.

At me and my space.
Tired of always taking the "safe" way.
Choosing trust.
Wanting to hook into love, snare and share it
    with someone.
I ponder, what will be required of me – with
    separation.
The wave of trust,
Suspended and holding.
Still no fear – anxiety – concern.

Is that – after all – the secret of life?
To let go and be tossed?
Like the molecules of water
In an ocean wave?
Like the dried leaf fallen,
driven by the wind to recycle
and be born again?
As a spring shower?
Or rose petal?

I feel tossed and driven, tugged and prodded.
Yet calm and at peace for the moment.
And moment by moment,
It shifts both mood and movement.
Affected and effecting events and people
Surrounding me still tossed and driven,

What power do I have but letting go?
To flow free, not bumping the shore,
Or captured in the dam
Of someone's design.
So now attachment to
Flow – must be let go
Bottom line, let go.

- 2001

LATHER, RINSE, REPEAT – BECOME

WHO KNEW SHAMPOO INSTRUCTIONS ARE SPIRITUAL POINTERS

A vacation is a lovely way to remember how much you love being home. At least, that's what I realized after coming back from Treasure Cay, Bahamas. Something about leaving for a while helps you see everything more clearly—the soft edges of your daily rhythm, the familiar corners of your space, the tiny comforts that quietly hold you together. But this time, I came back with more than appreciation for my house—I came back feeling deeply connected to the home I've built *inside*. The one made from choices, reflections, a few brave leaps, and a whole lot of rinse-and-repeat becoming.

That inner home didn't show up overnight. It arrived through layers—of noticing, of shedding, of returning to the same old questions from a slightly new vantage point. Again and again. Becoming, I'm finding, is not a dramatic one-time metamorphosis. It's a swirl. A slow spin. A loop that brings you back to the beginning with a little more softness and a lot more honesty. And like most cycles that matter, it rarely looks like progress until suddenly, it *is*.

The other day, I was going through old posts and journals, and I could see it—the threads of how I've become who I am now. Not all at once, but piece by piece. Some entries were hopeful. Others raw. Some full of fire, some foggy with doubt. But together, they revealed something steady underneath. The ongoing willingness to look again. To show up. To pause before reacting. To try the same practice *one more time*. Not because it didn't work the first time, but because every round teaches something different. Like circling a sculpture and seeing new shadows.

And here's the thing—it *is* a trail marker when you realize you're in that cycle. When you catch yourself revisiting something—not because you failed, but because you're ready to see it differently. That's a moment worth noticing. A quiet click in your becoming. When you don't race to be done, but return willingly. When you realize the loop isn't a setback—it's the signal that something's working. That's when you know: you're not lost. You're learning. Again.

This rhythm—observe, reflect, turn it over, return again—is baked into everything now. It's how I listen. How I create. How I live. And this morning, as I sat in that swirl of awareness, this poem dropped in fully formed. It felt like both a summary and an invitation. So, here it is: my ode to the non-linear, to the brave revisiting, to the sacred shampoo cycle of transformation.

Enjoy.

Becoming: Shake Well Before Use

"Wouldn't it be nice?" she sighs--
Then I could __________!
Then I would ________!
Then I'd feel ________!
Then I'd show _______!
Then I'd look ______!
Then I'd finally know _________!
Wouldn't that be lovely?

Read & re-read
that first stanza--
over & over & over.
Fill in the blanks.
OBSERVE—NOTICE—STAND.
DWELL—BROOD—SIT
in your words,
the images conjured,
the feelings & energy
flowing and weaving.

Step in—step out.
Walk 'round "it."

Take your time.
Rushing is resistance!
Fly over, float through,
turn it upside-down.
Swing back & forth,
forth & back--
again & again.

Just when you imagine
you've "got it"--
DIVE UNDER!
Root around,
SHOVEL—SIFT—SORT.
MUSE—MULL—REVOLVE.
Whisper wise words
& continue to wonder
at the ease & grace of "it."

Return again to stanza one.
LATHER—RINSE—REPEAT.
No hurry—not racing,
only living as witness.
Hold it gently—the texture
pressing against your thumb.
Turning it in your hand,
examining the colors,
the reflections—the spice.
Isn't "it" nice?!

Pore over "it" like water,
flowing into each nook & cranny.
And when you know it by heart--
start again at stanza one.
CELEBRATE—CONTEMPLATE—
    CONSIDER.
RETURN—REWIND—ENTWINE!
Until at last,

it's not just "nice"--
it's necessary.
It's already real.
And so I create & become.

- 2023

unity

THE WHOLE ENCHILADA

LANDMARK: NOTHING TO FIX

I've danced with *fearless* before. Back in 2003, a little truth whispered its way into my bones: *there is no evil.* I didn't shout it from the rooftops—but I lived it. Quietly. Like a secret handshake with the Universe.

But now? My DMGS (Divine Magical Guidance System) isn't whispering. It's practically singing backup vocals with glitter and jazz hands: *The world isn't even broken.* The poem that arrived today is the evolution. The sassier sequel. *Fix-Free* doesn't just remember *Fearless*—it builds on her shoulders, throws off the repair manual, and reminds me (again and again) that there's nothing to fix. Just something to love. Starting here.

> **Fix-Free**
> There's a lovely truth
> peeking out at me.
> I've sensed it before.
> The perspective is resurfaced.
> It's simple, repetitive--
> a brain-worm of a concept.
> Dismissively unfussy.
> Also divisive and delicate.
>
> **The world is not broken.**
> Five words.
> **There is no evil.**
> Four words.
>
> They topple & strangle
> our modern sensibilities,
> our entire perspective--
> of earth, of others--

of life now turned on its head.
Upside down,
backasswards,
swirling in *NOT SO!*

Forest, meet the trees.
Let it sink in, soak up.
What to do?
What to be?
If there is nothing
out there
to fix or fight,
fear or defend?

A concept so lovely—so alarming.
Are you, brave soul--
Horrified? Fearful?
Indignant? Upset?
Traumatized? Mortified?
Contemptuous? Superior?
Avoiding? Numb?
It is a rather harrowing,
bullshit-shattering,
grandiosity-wrecker
in four words or five.

What about those four little words--
did they even register?
There is no evil.
Does that spin you out?
Four tiny words,
mocking centuries
of fear-based morality,
punishment, and control.

Not saying harm doesn't happen--
but it changes the story.

It doesn't excuse.
But it transforms.
From blame to curiosity.
From attack to inquiry.
From righteousness
to real compassion.
That kind of shift?
Is dangerous.
And sacred.
And delicious.

Does it stir up any
individual responsibility?
Does it offer relief?
Hope?
Freedom?
What to do—create?
What to be—present?

The world is not broken.
Five words.
There is no evil.
Four words.

I have always prided
myself on my above-average
fixing, defending, proving,
being-right,
looking-good skill sets.
Until I realized I'd
LOST MYSELF
by casting a shadow so big
I couldn't see, literally,
the forest for the trees.

Shhhush now.
Far be it from me

to shatter the delusion
or interrupt the heartbreak, anxiety
judgement, and drama
you're so addicted to.
Forget it… never mind.

Shhhush. Shush now.
Turn the page—move along.
I won't defend or argue,
Convince or cajole.
You see the freedom,
you know the truth--
and it's our little secret.
Or you don't—yet.
It's all good.
Peace out.

- March 2025

We're not just talking politics, climate change, or central banking conspiracies (though, *chef's kiss* to that trifecta of existential dread). We're talking about **the whole enchilada**—our worldview, inherited myths, and the deep-seated belief that if we don't fix it all *right now*, everything goes to hell. But then comes the pause. The breath. That tiny turn inward. Your DMGS hums softly, and you remember —there's another way. It's uncomfortable at first, like coming out of the woods into bright sunlight. But then your soul's pupils dilate. Once your inner compass locks on, you can't unsee the truth. The world's not broken. You're not broken. And that fix-it compulsion? Just background noise.

Now rewind 20+ years when I was just learning to tune into my DMGS and the major static wasn't about fixing it was all about fear.

Fearless

Evil?
There is no evil.
I saw, I felt this truth this morning.
In the sky something lifted,
Like a cloud I couldn't see
and didn't know was there.
And light of a lighter quality
was present all around me.

And the burden of living in
subtle, constant,
nagging fear was lifted.

No fear of judgment, meeting strangers.
No fear of loss, meeting friends.
I choose not to give life to judgment, to loss.
Without my thought or breath,
they do not exist.

How will it be now?
To live each moment
as a precious gift of love?
Open – accepting,
observing and watching
for the opportunity to
give love back to all creation?
Even to me?

How will it be now?
To see the sweetness, the gentle lesson,
the good chance, pre-sent in each moment –
Just so I may remember who I Am?

How will it be now
To feel?
To laugh?
To love?
Without fear –
I am remembering.

- 2003

PART SIX

WHAT I LEARNED OFF TRAIL

WHEN CLARITY SHOWS UP IN THE WEEDS

Tales, reflections, and hard-won insights to elevate your own journey.

These are the wild cards. Not science, not scripture, and definitely not sponsored content—just the stuff that actually worked. Hard-won, sideways, sometimes poetic or politically incorrect, always personal.

These are the trail notes I scribbled after the map blew away. Truths that showed up when I stopped trying to impress the imaginary panel of judges in my head—and started listening instead.

Not inherited, not handed down, not data-backed—just lived. Tiny rebellions. Quiet pivots. Unexpected clarity found in the tall grass of real life.

You won't find them on a vision board, but they might just be the compass you didn't know you were holding.

DANGER
EXPECTATIONS
AHEAD

FANTASY FAMILY FUNERAL TOUR

FROM NORMAN ROCKWELL TO REAL LIFE

"Please just fill in your first name and stick the name tag on your left upper chest. Thanks so much—then I can see it easily when you're seated." I probably repeated that sentence thousands of times. I was the seminar leader. I even developed the course myself: PRIDE (People Respecting Individual Diversity Extravaganza). Decades ago —before diversity was a thing—I had insights and practices for being just a bit kinder and gentler to yourself and others. Extravaganza? Why yes, of course. It was NOT a "work" shop.

Part of the daylong experience included a closer look at what your values are. What can't you live without? Family. That was the answer. Frequently. Repeatedly. Honesty, God, and Love came up a lot too. I'd nod thoughtfully when people said "family," as if it were obvious. But it never felt obvious to me. I thought maybe I just didn't "get it." Or maybe it was something broken in me. Still, I led the exercise with conviction. That's the funny thing about teaching —you don't have to have it all figured out. You just have to create space for the truth to emerge.

Now, all these years later, I think I finally understand: I never actually rejected "family" as a value—I just confused it with a Disney fantasy. The truth that emerged recently had everything to do with my actual, local, right-in-front-of-me family experience. My father-in-law passed not long ago, and I had a front-row seat to what real, present-day family looks like—his wife, daughters, grandchildren, and friends all orbiting around him with care and presence. No drama. No resentment. Just wine, blankets, connection, love. All that attention and acknowledgment—it was a blessing to witness. And, if I'm being honest, a bit of a gut punch. Because while I watched all that connection unfold around him, part of me was thinking: That's what people mean when they say "family."

And just like that, I realized something: I hadn't rejected the value—I'd just been grieving the version of it I thought I was supposed to have. The fantasy family. The someday sisters. The effortless intimacy that never quite showed up. In the past, I would've spun out. Played the victim like it was my part-time job. Blamed everyone and their dog. I could've milked it for days—weeks—years, even. But I've since learned that blaming "the family" doesn't actually work. It doesn't get me anywhere new. In plain old business-speak: it's ineffective. The ROI on that kind of drama is abysmal. So, when that old inclination pops up, I treat it like a spam call: decline, delete, and move on. And truthfully, I didn't have a lot of tools back then. Emotional intelligence wasn't modeled. There was no communication—just silence. "No talk, no touch, no eye contact please!" could've been our family crest.

It reminded me of the often-hesitant women in my PRIDE seminars—sitting in small circles, nervously sharing truths they'd never considered before. Some proudly claimed family as their core value. Others whispered about Friendship, Joy, and other aspirational values they weren't quite sure they were allowed to want. And I always said: there's no right answer—only the one that's real for you. Turns out, that's the lesson I needed too. Not the value that sounds noble or looks good on paper. Not the one you inherited by default. And definitely not the one you stitched together in your head with a Norman Rockwell background mural and a backup theme song. Just the value that's real—for you.

So, I'll ditch the fantasy. Let go of the memo on how to act 'properly'—you know, the one no one ever actually got. Book the ticket. Go see my mom in September. This time, though, I'm doing it differently—not out of duty or guilt or some weird inherited script, but because I finally understand: I get to create what family means for me now. I get to shape the value of "family" with my one primary remaining blood relative—my mom. I don't have to follow anyone's definition. I can be intentional, tender, even bold about it. I can show up with care, with curiosity, and with an eye toward the future. I can build something that makes me feel more present, more connected, more free.

I had this strange old belief that I needed to include her new husband, like it would be rude not to. But… hello?! Permission granted. I get to have time with just her. I can whisk her away like a Thelma & Louise movie heroine with a convertible and a rockin' playlist.

Is it perfect? No. But it's personal, it's present, it's for real—and it's mine. Turns out, you don't need a fantasy family. Just a plane ticket, a mom who still answers your calls, the guts to be real, a playlist that doesn't include childhood trauma, and a well-earned, awake-and-aware gold star in Living My Actual Life—PRIDE-style.

Life after Death

Living on the edge
Of life and death
What will you do?
When will you hedge?
How much of what you do
Or don't do now, is rooted
In a tomorrow based
On fear, self-created?
Where will you sign
Or walk or stand?
What will you speak,
Or be, with design?
It leaves one hovering,
Distant and yet,
Intertwined deeply
In the moment.
Forget perfection,
And all you "trust" of reality.
It does not exist,
This is uncharted territory.
All you have to guide you
Is all you've never known,

And trust and faith and confidence
In talking to a stone.

- 2001

My image of Versailles with graphics by a friend… just for this poem.

DEAR LOVE: WTF ARE YOU?

WARNING: MAY CONTAIN TRAPDOORS & PERMISSION SLIPS

Eventually, I guess it finally happened. The dark grey, cloudy, chilly, cold, and damp outside weather navigated its way inside my head. Damn. It took a lot of meditation—and a healthy dose of sunshine—to finally snap me out of my doll drums. (Yes, doll drums. You read that right. Melancholy with a few pink sparkles and a pouty lip.)

I've been experimenting with a new morning meditation. One word. Love. That's it. Just a daily exploration of what love means *for me*. What does it feel like? How does it show up? What happens when I stop demanding that it look a certain way?

Like the word *God*, the word *Love* has been firmly parked on my internal "Use With Extreme Caution" list for a while now. Whether it was my original interaction with those words, or the way they've been hijacked, inflated, and twisted into cringe-inducing memes and overly idealistic frameworks—I had long since tossed them into the back of my metaphorical baggage bus. Still unpacked. Still heavy. Ready for an adventure I wasn't quite willing to take. And yet, apparently, both words are central—core even—if I want to fully live from and communicate with my DMGS (Divine Magical Guidance System). So, *fine*. I'll unpack *Love* first. Then maybe I'll peek at the other one. (*Maybe.*)

This new practice started about a week ago. I've been wandering Insight Timer like a curious mystic, searching for guided meditations that might offer a doorway—or even a doggie door—into a <u>felt sense of love</u>. Not the concept. The experience. To begin, I needed to narrow the field. I'd rather start with adjectives than synonyms. I mean, should I be looking at Love the noun? Love the verb? Geeze.

Here are a few obvious definitions that I've eliminated so far: A strong feeling of emotional attachment. An intense attraction or profound likeability. A person you love, respect, or lust after. A favorable inclination or enthusiasm for something. Reverence for someone or something. The act of engaging in coitus (sex). An intimate relationship between two people. Obsessional enthusiasm or extreme liking. Polite greetings or good wishes.

It was easy to eliminate all definitions that related to another person or that had attachment, obsession or coitus included. However, staring at definitions and dissecting usage just sent me into a tailspin. So instead, I dropped the dictionary and dropped in. I've used the meditations to feel what was already there, beyond the noise and associations. And here's what I found so far: I am not deficient in love. Not lacking, not empty. (I originally thought I had to "heal" something for love to flow.) This thing I'm calling Love—it's not scarce. It's not transactional. It's not earned or withheld or measured out like medicine. It is literally everywhere, all the time, without exception or doubt.

When I try to visualize love, the only info I receive is: BIG. POWERFUL. Unconditionally flowing. Always moving, always available. **Love isn't a feeling—it's a living field.** It moves through everything, responds to nothing, and welcomes it all.

One meditation was especially fun—it guided me through hallways and doors inside the "mind", leading to my personal library which comes fully stocked with every drop of wisdom the universe has ever offered—no late fees, no gatekeepers, just me and the infinite. I imagined mine nestled inside a great ancient tree, glowing and translucent like a greenhouse. I actually noticed a book titled LOVE and cracked it open, half-expecting something preachy or profound. Instead, it read like a permission slip: It radiated acceptance. No rules. No punishments. No criticisms. Just welcome mats in every direction. I had no idea what to do with that, so I sat there blinking—delighted and confused. To even *imagine* a space without the slightest hint of judgment was disorienting… and delicious. And it's _unconditionally indifferent_ to my choices.

That last bit startled me. Love isn't a mom coming to kiss a scraped knee. It's not reward or punishment, not approval or disapproval. It's not optimism or pessimism, not good or bad. It is *not* rooted in judgment, in any form. And yet, it's not apathetic either. It's not a shrug or a void. It's more like a presence that says: "I'm here. I've always been here. You can tap in whenever you want —but I'm not chasing you down." It nourishes when asked. Period. No preconditions. No history check. No future requirements. It doesn't care what I've done, am doing, or plan to do.

In the library of my mind, Love is the space itself. It's the hall and the shelves, the ceiling and the floor. It's the trapdoors and secret passageways behind the walls. Like the sky holds all clouds and all winds—rage storms and soft breezes alike—Love holds all I am, all I've been, and all I'm becoming. It's the container. The backdrop. The deep pulse of safety and trust that says: You're allowed. All of it. Always.

That's all for now, folks. If God is Love and I'm supposed to love my neighbor as myself, then learning to love *me* isn't extra credit— it's the whole enchilada. The adventure's off to a promising start as I finally get around to unpacking that dusty old trunk marked **LOVE**, tucked away in the back of my train—and apparently filed somewhere in my Multiverse Personal Library all along. Stay tuned. This one's worth seeing through.

Grateful Dread

What if joy overwhelms me?
What if gratitude floods and drowns me?
Is this righteous fear?
Can sweetness lay waste?
Will bliss conquer and bury me,
So far away I won't know
Where or who I am?

Is this noble terror?
Guiltless doubt?
Safety might smother?
Beauty could blind me?

Honesty may scorch,
Or flash and smolder forever deep down?
It is true, I can feel it.

And there's nothing for it.
Bliss is pain.
Tenderness - Torment.
Agony - Joy.
A trick of the triad.
A paradox of present-ness
And thankful, blameless fright.

- May 2009

WATER
IS
LOVE
L McC 11-15-24

OF WATER & COFFEE

ALIGNMENT, ONE CUP AT A TIME

Each afternoon the meditations I experience appear to be all the same. Life is a funny thing, isn't it? Even when it seems like nothing's new—bam! Heraclitus said it most clearly with his saying: "You can't step into the same river twice." Or in my case, you can't have the same meditation twice!

This idea of ever-newness hit me again during a recent meditation practice. The guided session (from an OSHO app—I call it BYOB: Be Your Own Bestie, is rooted in a course I recently completed: **OSHO Reminding Yourself of the Forgotten Language of Talking to Your BodyMind.** It's a 45-minute guided journey of listening to your body, inviting alignment, and waiting for messages about new behaviors to emerge. On November 14th, one message came through loud and clear: Water is Love.

The image of the water drop filled with hearts was as vivid as if someone had painted it on the inside of my eyelids. It spilled effortlessly onto paper later that day, the font for the words even appearing by "mistake." The message that came with it was equally vivid: It's OK to drink more water. Morning, evening, before meals, in between meals—water is LOVE!

Oh joy! A behavior I can get behind 1000%. I already love water. No disguises, no flavor additives—just pure, clean goodness. And here at Providence Lodge, our well water is practically liquid gold. Aside from coffee, water and iced tea are my go-to beverages. But now, with this added encouragement, I've been stepping up my water game, pouring a little more with each passing day.

Now let's talk about coffee for a second. Coffee and I? We've had a good run. I couldn't do without my Starbucks fix on the train ride to work in New York City, no way! But lately, it's like a clingy acquaintance who's overstayed their welcome. Sure, it was warm and exciting at first, but now it's all acidic vibes and nausea. I mean,

I powered through for old times' sake—what's one more cup, right?
—but even my body's over it.

Over the past week, I've noticed this shift. After 1.5 cups, I'd get that sour, acidic tummy feeling, sometimes a wave of nausea so strong it made me question my life choices. But did I stop? Of course not. Coffee is my guilty pleasure, my reward, my safety net. And let's not forget the epic caffeine withdrawal headaches waiting in the wings.

Then, something miraculous happened. I didn't finish my second cup. It sat there, abandoned, waiting to be emptied later in the day. Yesterday, I planned for one glorious cup, no more. And today? I couldn't even finish that. Somewhere in the blur of nausea and mindfulness, I realized my body had been gently weaning me off coffee without any declarations, control tactics, or rebellious backlash.

Healthy, natural behaviors are rising to the surface in their own time, with their own priorities, without me needing to force or dictate. This, my friends, is the dream. No guilt, no struggle—just ease and grace. My attachment to coffee feels unnecessary now, even a little silly.

And that's the beauty of listening to your body. It's not about micromanaging every little thing; it's about trusting that, given the space and attention, your body knows what it needs. For me, it started with water—a simple, loving shift—and its growing into something bigger: alignment.

So here I am, on day 9 of this BYOB (Be Your Own Bestie) 30 day meditation journey, embracing more water and less coffee. The transition feels surprisingly natural. My body's wisdom, it seems, has been there all along.

And you know what? It's fucking awesome.

Here's to more water, less coffee, and the joy of discovering that change doesn't have to be forced—it can flow, just like a river.

Take Me
Take me with you
when you go
down

out
around.
Remember me
I'm here
inside
outside
within,
without
Remember to
call
dial in
tune in.
Remember me
and take me
with you
when you go
inside
outside
around
the town
the house
the world
Remember me
I'm happy to be
happy with you.
Let's go together.
Remember me
we'll have fun
and live and love
forward
onion peeling
onward & upward
together
Take me.

- August 2017

IT'S ALL GRAVY

SAVOR THE FLAVORS

Urban Dictionary: "It's all gravy." Gravy is a sauce made from the juices of meat or vegetables and enhances the flavor of a meal. In leaner times, having gravy was a sign you had enough meat and vegetables to make such a thing—an indicator of richness and satisfaction. Hence, the phrase "on the gravy train," meaning life is well-supplied with good things, often money or ease. "It's all gravy," therefore, means there's an abundance of good things in a given circumstance. It doesn't mean everything's perfect or that a situation is necessarily pleasant—but it *does* mean you're in a place of overflow, not lack.

A: "We just secured a lucrative, open-ended contract with the supplier."

B: "It's all gravy from here on, boys."

Well, guess what? My life is well supplied, too—and I've got an abundance of good things. It's all gravy from here on.

Today is day 348 of 2024. Only eighteen days left in this wild, transformative year. It's been a helluva ride—unexpected twists, detours, cosmic speed bumps, and some secret shortcuts I didn't even know I needed. My guiding word for the year has been *FREEDOM*—a North Star I kept returning to, even when wandering through some gnarly inner terrain. Yesterday, during meditation, I received a set of messages that felt liberating. They weren't totally new—I've heard them before—but repetition is the secret sauce of real change. Like marinating. Insights need time to sink in, soak, and flavor the whole dish. Transformation doesn't come from flashy breakthroughs—it's in the slow simmer.

For something to truly change, it has to become more than a passing thought. It has to settle into the bones, reroute your reflexes, and become something you live, not just something you nod along with and forget. That takes time. And as always, there's no rushing the gravy. If someone tells you otherwise, they're selling shortcut slop. We're not microwaving meaning here—we're slow-cooking soul with real ingredients.

Earlier this week, I stumbled across a **Michael Singer podcast** titled *"Doing the REAL WORK to Free Yourself."* I didn't plan to listen; it just appeared like a cosmic breadcrumb. I pulled the transcript from YouTube, printed it (I AM that person—but you knew that), and let it speak. His message—simple, steady, and strong—landed with a surprising clarity. The metaphors weren't revolutionary, but something in how he said it—or where I was emotionally—clicked. Shifted something. Loosened something. He wasn't shouting; he was just pointing at the door. You don't rush freedom. And you don't give up—you stay curious.

Is it fair to say that everything changed and nothing changed? That everything matters and nothing does? That there's nothing to do—and yet everything is different? What's actually changed? Maybe it's just that I finally stopped trying to earn my life. That I don't need to prove I deserve peace. That it's always been gravy— and I just didn't know how to taste it. I feel clearer. Calmer. Less coiled. And—if I'm being bold—I feel *done* with self-improvement. I'm not here to be shinier, better, faster, or more palatable. I'm here to be me. No finish lines. No final boss. Just more me, moment by moment. Because freedom isn't the reward for doing the work—it *is* the work. It's not a perk, it's the point.

The past few weeks brought a bizarre injury—one of those out-of-nowhere hiccups that forces everything to a halt. Every morning I open the blinds on our tall windows, just a pull and up they go. But this time, *I* went down. Arms full, nothing to break the fall, I landed hard on my low back—feet and spine at a perfect 45-degree angle— flat on the floor. I laid there stunned, rocking, sobbing, and hissing "fuck" like it might call off the pain. It was more pain than I'd felt in decades—and over *nothing*. No trip. No slip. Just a tip. A tiny push backward from the Universe. "Oh, you don't appreciate what you've got? Here—have some appreciation for any movement, bending, lifting, or walking for the next two months." She waved her wand like a drunk fairy godmother and gave me a crack instead of a crown. And no—I wasn't in denial. I was just in shock. *WTF, Universe?*

Singer's core message was this: Learn to *handle it*. "It" being everything that happens—whether you like it or not. It rains on your birthday? It's not personal. Mother Nature doesn't give a shit about your cake. Be more like her. Stop writing cosmic conspiracy theories starring you as the victim. Handle what happens—don't add drama dressing and call it a spiritual journey.

So yeah. It's all gravy from here on. Not because life is suddenly easy, but because I've stopped expecting it to make sense or behave. I'm not here to be seen. I'm not here to win. I'm not even here to "grow" in a way that earns me gold stars or spiritual upgrades. I'm here to *taste*. To live like someone who knows the sauce is sacred. To savor even the lumps. Especially the lumps. Because this is it. This is the feast.

And I am not missing another bite.

With All My Senses
<u>Envision</u>, If you will
The most
Luxurious
Forest.
Deep green
Trees
Reaching for
The sun
Standing tall
Proud
And calm

<u>Hear</u>, If you can
The wind
Whispering.
Rustling
Ever so gently
Through the flora
Stirring them
Magically
Generating a

Symphony

<u>Feel</u>, If you may
Warm luminescent
Light
Peaceful and
Lusciously
Pulsing.
Bordering the
Cutting
Shadow's cool
Edge

Feel it
Aching?

<u>Smell</u>, If you dare
The forest
The wind
The light
And the shadow
Damp green
Dry warmth.
Vibrating

<u>Taste</u>, Unabashed
The spice
In the air
Let it taunt you
Sharpen your
Tongue
Grow your awareness
Savor calm
Delight in depth

Stop now,
My love,

And intensify
Each sense
Push every Limit,
Each
Boundary
Eliminate
Distraction

To me
You are
The forest
The breeze
The shadow
And the light.
You are the
Scent and flavor
I choose to explore
In this life

I love you with all my senses.

- 2014

PERCEPTION OF HEART

THE WISDOM OF THE WAVE

I've been practicing the release of lower-frequency emotions, as described by David R. Hawkins in his **Map of Consciousness**. It's given me a surprising sense of freedom—and a new lens for self-awareness. Also, naturally, another layer of cultural bullshit to explore. No wonder I'm so suspicious and cautious of people. The lowest levels to release include shame, guilt, apathy, grief, fear, desire (a HUGE one for me), anger, and pride. According to Hawkins—a scientist, not a chakra-doodling guru—these aren't just poetic descriptions. These emotions correspond to measurable energy frequencies emitted by the body. His work aims to eliminate suffering by examining how these suppressed energies affect our entire system. He writes: *"The elimination of suppressed emotions has a positive health benefit. It decreases the overflow of energy into the body's autonomic nervous system and unblocks the acupuncture energy system"* (p. xxii). Apparently, it's demonstrable by muscle testing—my fellow nerds can geek out accordingly.

Lately, I've been absorbing his book **Letting Go: The Pathway of Surrender**, alongside a daily audio course by **Dr. Debra Ford** called Daily Pulse on Insight Timer. She explores the Tao. The two bodies of work have gotten squished together and tossed around in my brain like an energetic smoothie, and I've started noticing some fascinating patterns. There are probably other influences mushed in there too—no matter. It's all good.

Here's what's risen to the surface so far:

- Suffering is caused by imbalances in the physical, mental, and emotional human system.
- An imbalance is essentially too much of one of two opposites. Balance is the even distribution of X that enables stability.

- Therefore, suffering comes from having too much or not enough of something—or the *perception* that that's the case.

The "perception" bit is key. Our perception determines our experience, regardless of the so-called truth of any given situation. (Can you tell I studied at a liberal arts school? Classic three-part logical framework here… with the built-in assumption that the first premise is true. Stay with me.)

Now this next bit might feel totally disconnected, but give it a minute—I'm coming around the bend.

What are the constants in the body? What mechanisms define physical balance? Breath and heartbeat. Without them, I wouldn't be here to ponder this stuff. The lungs expand and contract to move air. The heart does the same with blood. Both pump rhythmically, without needing my conscious approval. These cycles are the literal definition of life: full and empty, in and out, expansion and contraction.

Life is full of dualities—day and night, hunger and fullness, summer and winter, motion and stillness. And within me, the balance of urgency is calm. The balance of a busy mind is meditation. As I've learned to better discern illusion from truth, and peel away my own expectations and judgments, I've returned to that "middle space" again. The one I keep talking about. The observer's seat. The witness chair. The still place between the pendulum swings.

So where is the pump for emotions? What's the mechanism behind the invisible currents of feeling and energy? If air and blood have their rhythm, shouldn't there be one for this too?

Turns out—there is. But unlike the heart or lungs, this one is more influenced by illusions and beliefs. It's electrical and measurable, but far less obvious to the naked eye. *And here's the kicker:* just like the others, it's meant to *flow*. It's not meant to hold. You wouldn't try to store a breath permanently. You'd pass out. Same goes with feelings. But I've noticed how easily I attach meaning to them, spin stories around them, and hold on way past the natural exhale.

That's where the real suffering lives.

The feelings themselves are usually brief—grief, anger, shame—they surge and then, if left alone, they shift. But when I start spinning blame, brewing injustice, grasping for purpose or identity, I turn those natural frequencies into a full-blown flood. I override the system. I resist the flow. I stop stopping. Or I stop letting go. Either way—it's unnatural.

What helps me most is remembering: I am not a container. I'm a conduit. The emotion isn't stored inside me. It moves *through* me. Like music through a speaker. Like wind through a flute. (Yes, Rumi, I hear you: "I am the hole in the flute that the Christ's breath moves through." Still works.)

This helps with the guilt too. I used to worry that I'd carry grief forever. But now I wonder—what if it's not meant to be "carried"? What if it's just a vibration playing out? A note finishing its echo?

When I can stop interfering, emotions pass. And then, something new begins. I've come to believe this is what "wisdom of the heart" really means. Not sentiment. Not sweetness. But rhythm. A heart expands and contracts. It doesn't beat continuously in one direction. The wisdom is in the wave, not the still point.

So my job isn't to control the tide. It's to stop building dams. To pause long enough to allow the flow. To feel what moves through without attaching to it—or worse, identifying *as* it.

And that brings me to another question I've been chewing on: How do I continue releasing the decades of suppressed emotion already clogging the system? Because even if I stop the new traffic, there's still a backlog or bottle neck…

For now, I'm staying curious. Reading Hawkins. Exploring the Tao. Practicing the pause. I'm starting to believe my emotions aren't evidence of brokenness or danger. They're just weather. Temporary, natural and necessary.

Somewhere deep inside, I already know how to ride the waves. I've just been holding my breath.

Balance

So light and airy
So deep and churning
To discover the mean

To tread the tight rope
With courage and style,
No fear here

Swimming in thoughts
Drowning in desire
My life's passion
Haunts me – gleaming.

- 2001

Obsess, Resist, Rewire:
This is NOT A Wellness Plan!

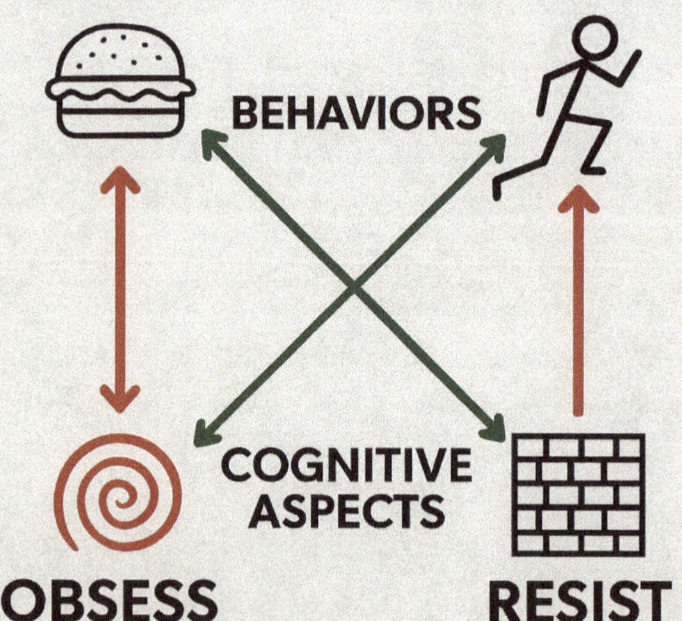

OBSESS.
RESIST. REWIRE.

THIS IS NOT A WELLNESS PLAN

This diagram was surprisingly challenging to create. You know that feeling when something makes perfect sense in your head? It's clear, intuitive, almost like a dance. Then, you try to capture it on paper, and suddenly it's boxes and arrows and scribbles. That was my experience with this meditation insight. I started with a big swooshy arrow, feeling like an artist in flow, and ended up with... a visual puzzle that looks more like a science project.

During meditation, I pictured a big swooshy arrow—blue and curling—representing a simple shift from one set of thoughts and behaviors to a radically different experience of the same things. The swooshy arrow was the perfect representation of this shift I felt—something light, effortless, that just swoops in and transforms everything in its path. It's the kind of arrow that says, "Hey, no need to overthink this." It was more about the feeling of letting go than about any specific outcome.

So why, you might ask, did it turn into a diagram with boxes, labels, and lots of arrows? There's something about human nature that loves making simple things complicated. We have an epiphany and immediately start dissecting it. Can we just let the swooshy arrow be? Apparently not. We want diagrams, explanations, and flowcharts. The meditation experience said, "Just shift your focus." But of course, I had to go and create a map for it.

And that map? It's all about flip-flopping behaviors. The concept sounds elegant: instead of obsessing over food, I could obsess over movement. Instead of resisting movement, I could try resisting certain foods. It's like rearranging furniture in your mind—familiar elements, just with a new layout. There's something oddly freeing in realizing you don't have to "get rid of" anything; you just move things around. For once, I don't have to "fix" anything; I just need to try placing it somewhere else.

So, how do we actually make this work? I started small. When I noticed myself obsessing over food—what I ate, what I planned to eat—I paused and asked, "What would it look like to use this energy on movement?" It's like rewiring a circuit in my brain. I remind myself that I can simply shift my focus, that I can experiment with where I put my mental energy. The more I practice, the more natural it becomes.

Meditation creates this space of non-judgment—a place where all these "undesirable" behaviors suddenly feel neutral, even kind of interesting. From that space, it's easier to look at them objectively and say, "What if I just moved things around?" Instead of trying to exile certain habits, I can simply shift their energy. The openness I felt during meditation allowed me to see that I don't need to judge myself for having these tendencies. They're just part of the puzzle.

And sometimes, the simplest insights turn out to be the hardest to capture on paper. It's funny, isn't it? We use every ounce of brain power to expect, search, judge, and compare, only to discover that a single swooshy arrow might hold the key. Whether or not I get this "flip-flop" idea working in real life, I get to keep exploring, moving things around until it feels right. That's progress in itself.

So here's to the swooshy arrow—a symbol of simplicity, ease, and trust. I may have turned it into boxes and arrows, but the insight remains. Sometimes, the solution doesn't need to be complex. Sometimes, a little swoosh is all we need to rewire our experience.

Watering Plants

I think I'll water
The plants today.
And take a moment
And say hello.
I'll use the smallish
Watering pot.
It takes many trips

But that's ok.
Because I'm watering
The plants today.

I'll prune
And pluck
And fluff
And pet.
One by one
It is enough.
Pot by pot
Leaf by leaf
Caring.

Such a gift!
I'm grateful
To water
Plants today.
That is all.

Oh! And…perhaps,
A lesson grand.
For me to find
For all times
I'll remember
As I'm watering.
Oops, just did!
Magical!

- December 2016

SCREW THE GRIND. TRUST THE FLOW.

SKILLS FROM SWIMMING IN THE DEEP END

Is it true that "what goes around, comes around"? Maybe—if you believe it. Is karma for real? I'm curious—if it is, how does it really work? Are there hidden laws of nature at play beneath the surface? Absolutely! These invisible forces—the ebb and flow of life, the tides of energy, and the subtle threads that connect us—remind me that there's always more than meets the eye.

What I do know is this: seasons happen. People, thoughts, and emotions appear and disappear in waves. The ebb and flow of motivation and inspiration is undeniable in my personal experience. In the past, whenever I encountered an ebb, my knee-jerk reaction was always to resist, push through, and never give up. But isn't that the opposite of "going with the flow"?

Living one block from the ocean on Venice Beach, California, taught me a lot about the rhythm of the tides. I'd watch waves advance and retreat, each one flowing farther up the shore or pulling back, depending on the tide. I witnessed ferocious storms and times of total calm.

I remember a specific ebb during my career when I tried to push through a project that simply wasn't ready. I poured my energy into every detail, ignoring the growing resistance I felt inside. The result? Burnout and frustration. Nothing flowed. I endured the pain, forced the progress, and achieved absolutely nothing of value. That whole "no pain, no gain" mantra? Total bullshit. Flow yields more fruit than force ever could. And gain doesn't have to hurt.

Later, when I paused and gave myself space, the clarity I'd been searching for arrived effortlessly. The lesson was clear: sometimes, flow comes only when we stop forcing it. Patience—and awareness —are the only salves for this particular force of nature.

I've witnessed my own ebbs and flows of emotion and inspiration. In these moments, I sometimes sense the faint pull of a thread beneath it all, connecting the waves of life and guiding me forward. Sometimes pushing through yields fruit; other times, it doesn't. Learning when to push and when to stand still feels like a hallmark of an ever-expanding maturity.

There are milestones, landmarks, and defining moments along the way, certainly. But the fall back and regroup often feels like an automatic, wild response to moving forward. "Two steps forward, one step back..." The pause—whether caution, contemplation, or simply waiting—is what allows me to be unattached. Given my intention and my actions, I can watch the outcome unfold and reflect: Was it even close to what I intended? The "step back" becomes a space to learn and grow with ease, little by slowly.

Though I don't have children, I often imagine what a curriculum in Life Skills might look like. What lessons would I teach my younger self? Lessons that allow the confident spirit to shine, creativity to flow, and life to be free of suffering (if not pain). After a 30-year corporate career training adults, I wonder how I could package my experiences to be touching, moving, and inspiring for peers—or for anyone seeking a little more ease in navigating life's ebbs and flows.

One of the first lessons I'd teach would be patience. It's a skill that doesn't come easily, especially in a culture of "hustle" and "no pain, no gain." Screw that. Patience is what allows me to ride the waves of life with grace. Another would be awareness—the ability to set aside beliefs, expectations, and defensiveness, to stop blaming or criticizing, and instead to fully experience the moment as it is. Awareness invites me to notice life's tides as they shift and pivot gracefully, rather than reactively. Both skills have carried me through countless moments of uncertainty, showing me how to trust the process rather than fight it.

And at the heart of it all, I'd include a lesson about connection—about learning to recognize and follow the subtle threads that guide me. There's an emerald thread of the soul that runs through my life, quiet but persistent, and noticing it is what allows me to navigate even the stormiest tides. This awareness creates space for trust, curiosity, and growth.

For some time now, I've shared my journey and reflections here, inspired by images and ideas from my daily meditation practice. Recently, though, that hasn't felt adequate—or entirely authentic. But in writing this, I've noticed a thread running through my tapestry, one that might just resonate with others.

This thread—the emerald thread of the soul—has always been there, even if I wasn't looking for it. It's a thread that's shown up in moments of inspiration, in quiet pauses, and even in the middle of life's storms. Following it has taught me to see the beauty in small, subtle moments and to trust that even the "setbacks" are a critical and necessary part of a larger picture.

Each individual experience may or may not resonate or inspire you, but the bright emerald thread of the soul is beginning to emerge. This is what I'll pay attention to—watching for it out of the corner of my eye. It might not be visible immediately, but like the rising tide, it will eventually and inevitably raise all vessels.

The tide doesn't hustle. It doesn't grind. It doesn't chant toxic slogans like "no pain, no gain." The tide just *rises*. Quietly. Faithfully. And when we stop fighting and start flowing, we rise with it. This is the kind of trust I aim to embody in my own life: a steady faith that even when I can't see the full picture, the tide is lifting me toward clarity, growth, and alignment.

Myself

I am now and always will be
Myself

Who is myself?
Compassionate
Optimistic
Caring
Intelligent
Crazy
Aware
Thoughtful

How do I know this About myself?
I see pain and figure a way to let it go
I know the most extraordinary result is
    possible
I understand your pain
I can figure out how to make it better
Absurdly unusual solutions are best
I am witty and cognizant of the effects of
    everything
On everything
Amazing how aware and thoughtful
are similar in definition…
I would posit that thoughtfulness is awareness
manifested in kind deeds.

I know myself to be sneaky as well
And rebellious and self-sabotaging
Powerful and revolutionary
Not of this place

So non compliant
To the rules for a reason.

- 2011

Freedom Rocks
L A McCauley 2024

PART SEVEN
WHAT NOW? KEEP GOING!
ABOVE GROUND? YOU'RE STILL IN IT. DON'T STOP NOW.

You've come this far. The pack's lighter. The view's clearer. But the journey? Oh honey—it's nowhere near over.

This isn't a conclusion—it's a *launch*. These references, stories, practices, and resources explore what's possible after the "aha," when the practices start living in your bones and the voices in your head finally start sounding like allies instead of critics.

This is where you start trusting your gut a little more, turning down the volume on the fear-monger, and maybe—just maybe—pushing up that next trailhead with a little more courage (and maybe a little glitter). Whether it's following a link, taking a class, planting something, or finally signing up for that race car experience —you know the nudge. Follow it.

Further exploration doesn't mean *doing* more. It means living with more honesty, more depth, and more trust in your own rhythm.

We're not looping back.

We're spiraling forward.

Let's see where this leads.

You good?
good?
Yup.

ACCOUNTABILITY PARTNERS

CHEERLEADERS IN CHILL MODE

Wondering what an Accountability Partner even is?

It's just a human with a phone. That's it. Call it a Check-In Buddy, Progress Pal, Habit Homie, or Text-to-Trust Sidekick. Someone willing to give you a thumbs-up emoji when you report in about whatever promise you're currently keeping to yourself—like your meditation streak, movement goal, no-snacking experiment, or journaling practice. They don't coach you, guilt you, or give you gold stars. They just… exist. With thumbs.

———

Don't Know Where to Start?

Pick someone sympathetic to your goal—low-drama and reliable. Ideally, someone who isn't trying to fix you. You send a quick check-in: "Did my 10 mins," or "Day 3 complete." They respond with something simple—"Nice!" or "You go!"—or even just an emoji. If a few days go by without a ping, they might nudge you with a "Still on?" or a "You okay?" in case you fell off a cliff or got swallowed by chaos. (It happens.) If you fall off the wagon, just jump back on—after you consider what was working, what wasn't, and what needs tweaking. Maybe you started with 20-minute goals and now realize 2–5 minutes is way more doable. That's not failure —it's wisdom. Get real, don't give up. Adjust and continue. Flexibility, creativity, and consistency are the payoff *and* the practice.

Why Bother with Accountability Anyway?

- **It keeps you honest.** Saying something out loud—or typing it to your check-in buddy—makes it *real*. Suddenly you're not just *thinking* about meditating or journaling… you're doing it. Or at least thinking twice before bailing.
- **You act differently when someone's watching.** You act differently when you know someone might notice—even if they never say a word. Apparently, the faint possibility of being seen is enough to keep me from sliding back into low-effort mode. Turns out, minimal accountability is shockingly effective.
- **It's sneakily intimate.** You start with "Did my walk" and before you know it, you're trading memes, venting about your in-laws, or celebrating 7 days straight of not emotionally face-planting into a bag of chips. Magic.
- **Support doesn't need a pep talk.** Sometimes it's just a thumbs-up that says, "You showed up." No advice. No spreadsheet. No gold star. Just a little acknowledgment from another human in the arena. Weirdly powerful.
- **The real secret?** Accountability partners work *because* they're simple. Not because they fix you. Not because they're perfect. But because they remind you: you don't have to go it alone—even when the "it" is flossing or remembering to eat breakfast.
- **The key?** Keep it human. Keep it kind. And let it evolve to match where you are. No need to scale Everest —just text someone when you walk up the damn hill.

————

Try This Field Guide Moment:

Pick one small thing you've been *meaning* to do (but keep skipping). Think: daily meditation, drinking water before coffee, 5-minute journaling, walking around the block.

Now text a friend:

"Hey. I'm trying something new. Will you be my Check-In

Buddy for a week? No fixing, no advice—just shoot me a 👍 if I check in. If I ghost, feel free to poke me."

Then _do the thing_. Report back.

Bonus points if you add:

"Also, I hereby give myself permission to bail, change it, or fail gloriously and start again next Monday."

———

FIELD GUIDE RULE #17: ACCOUNTABILITY ONLY WORKS IF IT'S ROOTED IN HONESTY AND KINDNESS. NOT DELUSION AND GUILT.

———

More "Accountability Partner" synonyms for your inspiration and amusement:

- Check-In Buddy
- Progress Pal
- Goal Whisperer
- Trail Text Companion
- Kindness Mirror
- Sanity Sync
- Witness With WiFi
- Encouragement Echo
- Reminder Fairy
- Honest Hype Person

SAY
IT OUT
LOUD
I AM
EROUGH
I
TRUST
MYSELF

AFFIRMATIONS, MANTRAS, SPELLS & MOMENTS

WORD ALCHEMY: RELAX - REMEMBER - RELEASE

Wondering where prayer fits into this bit?

Me too. For years it felt too churchy, too loaded, or like something I needed a special robe or approval for. Eventually, I realized what I really needed was *language*—words I could say out loud (or in my head) to calm the chaos, shift my state, or hand something over. That's what this section is about: the homemade, heart-wired language tools I use to reset, release, and remember who the hell I am.

Welcome to your very own remix of prayer—Field Guide–style. Whether you call it a mantra, affirmation, spell, or mental Post-it note, this is language that *works*. Bonus: it also doubles as instant inspiration for your Arts & Crafts section. (You're welcome, future collage project.)

———

Don't Know Where to Start?

Try this: notice what you say to yourself on repeat. If your internal voice is all blame, fear, and judgment ("Why aren't you better by now?" "You always screw this up" "Be afraid, be very afraid!), then **you already have a mantra**—it just sucks. So let's write better ones. You don't have to be poetic. Just honest. I call these little tools by many names:

- *Set Aside Spells* (when I'm letting go)
- *Mantras* (when I need anchoring)
- *Affirmations* (when I'm shifting patterns)

• *Moments* (when I just need to pause and say something kind)

Pick your favorite. Or don't name it at all. Just write something that feels true or aspirational and *say it*. Bonus points if you write it in Sharpie on your wrist.

————

Why Bother with These Word Tools Anyway?

- **Because your brain is listening.** What you repeat becomes the background music of your nervous system.
- **Because words have weight.** When you speak them out loud, they carry clarity and vibration.
- **Because you deserve better scripts.** The old programming—criticism, control, shame—wasn't written by your soul. This is your rewrite.
- **Because creation starts here.** A phrase can become a seed. Say it enough, and eventually it grows into how you treat yourself, how you move through the world, how you *believe*.

————

FIELD GUIDE RULE #7: WORDS ARE SPELLS. USE WISELY. CURSE GENTLY.

————

Try This Field Guide Moment:

Write a **Set Aside Spell**. Use this format (or make up your own):

"I set aside [insert mental crap: judgment, comparison, fear, control, guilt]. In exchange for [insert the good stuff: calm, joy, clarity, courage, compassion, curiosity, softness, presence, peace]."

Example:

"I set aside my spinning thoughts, my expectations of how it 'should' look,

and my obsession with getting it right. In exchange for grounded-ness, grace, and a smidge of wonder."

Now write it up, type it out, print, add stickers, laminate it, or decoupage it to a mason jar. This is where Arts & Crafts meets Self-Talk Alchemy. Scatter them around your home like kindness land-mines—ready to explode in your favor.

———

FIELD GUIDE RULE #22: SAY IT OUT LOUD. YOUR CELLS ARE LISTENING.

DREAM
vision
BRAVE
BEGIN
CREATE
CREATE
BEGIN

ARTS & CRAFTS (YESSS!)

I GIVE YOU PERMISSION TO MAKE A MESS!

Wondering why a glue stick can feel like a liberation device?

This is the magic of making—whether it's signage with a message, flow painting, gardening chaos, intentional photography, or any tactile, creative pursuit. Think of creativity as imagination, inventiveness, originality—your way of forming something brand-new, physical or not. Maybe it's a rock garden on your windowsill with all the crystals you bought but can't remember the name or vibe of. Doesn't matter. The point is: it's *yours*.

———

Don't Know Where to Start?

Give yourself *time*. Slow down. Let it be relaxed, fun, and playful. Create a zero-pressure, zero-comparing, zero-judgment zone. I use a Set Aside Spell to start:

"I set aside all my insane expectations of perfection, beauty, or whatever I'm stuck on. I set it all aside in exchange for fun, open-minded curiosity, willingness, and wisdom."

Start there. Then grab whatever you've got—paper, a stick of glue, a handful of weeds. This is trial and error. You might love it, hate it, or discover that coloring outside the lines still pisses off the perfectionist in your head. Good! Try something else. Keep going until something clicks. **HAVE FUN.**

———

Why Bother with Creative Play Anyway?

- **It calms your frazzled nervous system.** There's something about gluing, doodling, digging, or finger-painting that brings the body and mind into the same room. Mood = lifted.
- **It lets you say the stuff you don't have words for.** Splotchy paint and stick figures are legit forms of therapy. You don't need talent. You just need permission.
- **It builds badass confidence.** Finishing a project—no matter how weird or wobbly—lights up the part of your brain that says "Hey, I *can* do stuff." Plus, making things by hand has been linked to slowing cognitive decline, boosting memory, and improving mood.
- **It reclaims play.** When you stop making it about being "good" or "artistic," you open the door to delight, surprise, color, texture, and freedom. No judge. Just joy.

———

Try This Field Guide Moment:

Pick a mantra. Any mantra. Or just pick a word.

Make it one that *means something to you*—maybe it's powerful, moving, grounding, funny, or slightly defiant. Whatever lights you up or snaps you out of a funk. Your word can be obvious and inspiring like **TRUST** or **ENOUGH**, or something more personal and weird (those are my favorite). I love acronym-based words that carry secret power. Like **RED**—which, for me, means "Don't React, Engage, or Defend." And yes, I made art out of it. Big gold letters. Red slash. It works.

Want help brainstorming? Grab your phone and open the **Word Hippo** app. Plug in your word and explore synonyms, opposites, rhymes, or surprising connections. It's a gold mine.

Once you've got your word (or phrase or acronym), break out the markers, paints, paper, stickers, whatever you've got. Make it big. Make it weird. Make it fun. Let Self Talk Alchemy meet Arts and Crafts magic.

Then hang it somewhere you'll see it—or stash it somewhere for future-you to discover. A bathroom mirror. The glove box. Laminated and hidden in your sock drawer.

This is you talking back to your habits. In color. In code. In kindness. My art projects are scattered throughout the book feel free to be inspired!

A WAY WITH WORDS
On Bein
FIELD GUIDE
FIELD GUIDE
SACRED WTFs
WILD FICTION
SC-FI
WILD FICTION FICTION
A WAY WITH WORDS

BOOKS AND THE BUZZ OF OUTSIDE WISDOM

PRE-PROCESSED INSIGHTS. DMGS FILTER RECOMMENDED

Wondering what qualifies as "resource" reading these days?

Pretty much anything that shifts your perspective, softens your heart, or knocks you lovingly off your habitual path. Sci-fi, self-help, sacred texts, wild fiction, audiobooks, or podcasts that make you belly laugh or finally feel seen. For years, ***This American Life Prairie Home Companion***, ***On Being, The Splendid Table,*** and ***A Way With Words*** were my soul food—weekly radio rituals turned podcast lifelines that kept me grounded while I wandered the country. If it sinks in, keep it. Now I tune into **Michael Singer** and **Eckhart Tolle** *once in awhile* as well. Thank you, authors, inspirers —whomever you are.

Don't Know Where to Start?

Let your curiosity lead—but skip the pressure to turn everything into homework. Books and podcasts can be daily anchors, trail markers, or the break you didn't know you needed. I do podcasts (or music) when my hands are busy—driving, gardening, cleaning. And sometimes, let's be real, I just want someone else's story in my ears while I sweep crumbs off the counter or wander the neighborhood in my flip flops.

Here's the key: *use discernment.*

Not everything is meant for you—and that's a good thing. If something feels heavy, hollow, or hijacks your peace, toss it back in the stream. Your intuition knows. Watch for the weird, follow the spark, and stay curious.

If it makes you feel like you need to fix yourself, buy twelve more courses, or overhaul your personality by Tuesday? Maybe not. There's no gold star for consuming more content. There *is* value in choosing wisely and knowing when to pause.

Why Bother with Books & Podcasts Anyway?

- **Because you don't have to reinvent the wheel.** Plenty of wise minds have left breadcrumbs—books, ideas, and insights that still ring true. My liberal arts education introduced me to the Great Books, and I'm glad it did. Don't ignore what's already been offered. If something shifts your perspective, softens your heart, or makes you laugh out loud—sci-fi, sacred texts, self-help, or stand-up—take it in. If it sticks, keep it. Thank you, elders.

- **Because it's basically time travel.** Ancient texts, modern insights, forgotten truths—all distilled into something that can land right in your now. Crazy how that works.

- **Because your inner guide can use a translator.** Sometimes the DMGS speaks through a line you underlined five years ago or a podcast episode your friend randomly shared. That book you almost didn't buy? Might be divine delivery.

- **Because sometimes joy is the whole damn point.** Re-read your favorite mystery or dog-eared romance novel (yes, the ones with the cheesy covers and "clutching" verbs). Or queue up that podcast where someone rants about squirrels. If it lifts your mood or makes you cackle, that's soul fuel.

- **Because potty books are the bomb.** I keep a carefully curated basket of 365-quotesy type books beside the toilet—and let me tell you, glorious moments are had by all. Mini wisdom hits or journalling inspiration while doing my business? Yes, please.

———

Try This Field Guide Moment:

Can you think of three books that changed something real in you—lit a spark, opened a portal, made you cry in the grocery store aisle? Do you still own them? Digital or physical, doesn't matter—just get your hands on one. Take a breath. Open the book at random or scroll with your eyes closed and stab the screen dramatically. Land on a sentence, a word, an idea.

Did it "re-mind" you of something important? Is it worth writing down and sitting with? Did it answer a question or give you goosebumps? Did you laugh or cry? No, nothing? Try again. Because sometimes magic needs a second chance or a different book.

FIELD GUIDE RULE #4: THOUGHTS WELCOME. ATTACHMENT NOT ADVISED.

THE
SPIRIT
ANIMAL
ORACLE
COLETTE BARON-REID

DEAR DECK WHATTSS UPP???

Wondering what a "deck" even is?

Playing cards date back to 9th-century China, and tarot cards have been used for insight and reflection since at least the 1400s. Turns out, pulling a card to get out of your own head is a timeless tradition—and it's stuck around for a reason.

Oracle decks, tarot cards, animal spirit cards—whatever format you prefer—they're just tools. Tools that help you pause, listen inward, and access what your DMGS already knows. Pull a card when you need a shift in perspective, a little validation, or a tiny nudge from the mystery. You don't need to believe in magic. You just need a question and a little curiosity.

Don't know which deck to start with?

Easy. Pick the one that makes you grin, raise an eyebrow, or mutter "oh please" while secretly feeling intrigued. That's your deck. Bonus points if it calls you out lovingly and occasionally makes you laugh-snort.

And hey—this is also a chance to practice the pause. Check your motive, just for a moment. Are you trying to prove something? Look good? Be right? (Be honest—your DMGS will know.) If not, then the one you pick will always be right. Even if it's weird. Even if it's not the "cool" one.

Or skip the Amazon shopping cart altogether and just use the deck(s) you already own. Yes, even that one that's been collecting dust. You might be surprised what it has to say now that you're actually listening.

Why Bother with Decks and Cards?
  • **Pattern interrupt.** Whether you're spiraling in thought, drowning in feelings, or just staring into space hoping for a clue—pulling a card is a helpful distraction. It shifts your focus to something intentional instead of whatever chaos your mind was feeding you. Basically: pause, shuffle, breathe. Already better.
  • **Offers a fresh lens.** A single word or image can crack open a window in a stuffy room full of your own recycled thoughts. A card doesn't fix things—it reframes them. And sometimes that's all the momentum you need.
  • **Creates ritual and intention.** You don't have to light candles (but go ahead if that's your vibe). The act of pulling a card is a sacred pause. It's a doorway to presence, a moment of "I'm listening now."
  • **Validates inner nudges.** Let's be honest—at least half the time you already know. But when a card shows up with the exact phrase or vibe you were just thinking about? That's the DMGS whispering: "You're not crazy. You're paying attention."
  • **Encourages self-reflection.** Cards don't always land perfectly—and that's part of the magic. Whether they resonate, confuse, or annoy you, they give you a mirror. You can sit with it. Or not. *(Pro tip: pulling a second card is not cheating. It's… exploring.)*
  • **Connects you to your DMGS.** This isn't about giving your power away—it's about engaging your inner knowing with a tangible ally. Pulling cards regularly builds trust in your own symbolic language. It's like chatting with your bestie... only this one speaks in metaphors, archetypes, and cosmic sass.

SHOUT OUT: to some of the best decks I've ever tried—all written by ***Colette Baron-Reid*** and brought to life by the stunning artists she collaborates with. These oracle cards are straight-up portals to insight and joy:

• **Spirit Animal Oracle** – A pocket-sized guide that taps into the wisdom of the natural world. It's like having spirit-animal road signs right in your hand, whispering reminders of who you are and where you're heading.

• **Wisdom of the Oracle Divination Cards** — Everyday insight in a 52-card format for love, growth, and grounding.

These decks aren't kitschy—they're classy portals with depth, humor, and gorgeous artwork. If you've ever wondered, *"Does Spirit have a sense of whimsy?"*—yes. Yes it does.

So, Dear Deck, THANK YOU. For the guidance, the laughs, the reminder that we're not walking alone or without wonder. If you're looking to bring a bit of oracle-magic into your daily field guide, start here.

You can pull cards online as well… here's a sample I just did:

DID YOU
CATCH
THAT?

LIFE HAPPENS – WATCH FOR IT!

AWARENESS AS A WITNESS CHANGES EVERYTHING.

Wondering What You're Supposed to Be Looking For?

You don't have to book a retreat or decode a dream journal to be in the middle of something sacred. You already are. Life is always talking. The question is: are you listening? Are you watching for the little nudge, the offhand comment, the random sign that loops back around at the perfect time?

If this guide has taught me anything, it's this: **revelations hide in the repeatable.** In the grocery store. The daily walk. The weird playlist shuffle. The red light. The eye roll. The neighbor's dog that always barks at just the right moment to wake me up. *Awareness turns the ordinary into insight. And insight? That's the power position.*

———

Don't Know Where to Start?

Start here: Pretend it *all* matters. That nothing is wasted. That the weird shit and the repetitive routines are not obstacles, but invitations. *Awareness isn't passive. It's participation.*

Look for:

- The number 11 or any number that you happen to see / notice multiple times a day.
- The song lyric that echoes your exact thought.
- The stranger who says something that sounds like it was meant just for you.
- The gut punch of déjà vu.

- The thing you keep saying you'll do "someday"… and it pops up three times in one week.
- That moment where your eyes catch something *ordinary*, but you feel it land as holy.
- Repetition. Loops. Quotes. Animal sightings. Tech glitches. Yes, even the annoying ones. (Especially the annoying ones.)
- That perfectly-timed moment that feels like a wink from the Universe. (Literally. "God winks" are a thing. Thanks, **SQuire Rushnell**.)

———

Why Bother with Awareness Anyway?

- **It builds your internal radar.** The more you notice, the more you *notice*. Awareness is a muscle—and it gets stronger with use. You start catching the micro-nudges before they snowball into drama.
- **It breaks the autopilot trance.** Wakefulness isn't about being serious. It's about being *present*. Watching for small wonders keeps you out of doom-scroll mode and in "Huh… that's interesting" mode.
- **It invites your DMGS to speak up.** Not as backup, but as the steady presence actually at the wheel. Awareness puts *you* in the co-pilot seat—where you can observe clearly, choose consciously, and stop reacting like a parrot on fire.
- **It's the seat of all power.** Without awareness, you're just reflex. Scripted. Repeating what you've heard, mimicking what you've seen, and reacting based on what you've never questioned. With awareness, you get to *pause*. You get to *pivot*. You get to *decide*.
- **It rescues meaning from the mundane.** Laundry can be a meditation. Errands can be a mirror. Conversations can be portals. Even your routines hold gold… if you're paying attention.

- **It keeps you from chasing glitter.** Some synchronicities are real pointers. And if the timing feels too perfect to ignore? That might be what author SQuire Rushnell calls a "God wink"—a little love note from the Universe disguised as coincidence. The phrase was spotlighted in an episode of *A Way with Words*, which just feels like confirmation wrapped in wink.

———

Field Guide Moment: Stay Curious, Not Cuckoo

For the next 48 hours, treat your life like a scavenger hunt. Don't change anything. Just *notice*.

What repeats? What catches your attention? What phrase, song, or symbol shows up more than once?

Jot down your own breadcrumbs. Not to solve anything. Just to notice. Awareness is the practice. Meaning will sort itself out.

FIELD GUIDE RULE #9: IF YOU SPOT IT, YOU'VE GOT IT. THAT'S AWARENESS. THAT'S POWER.

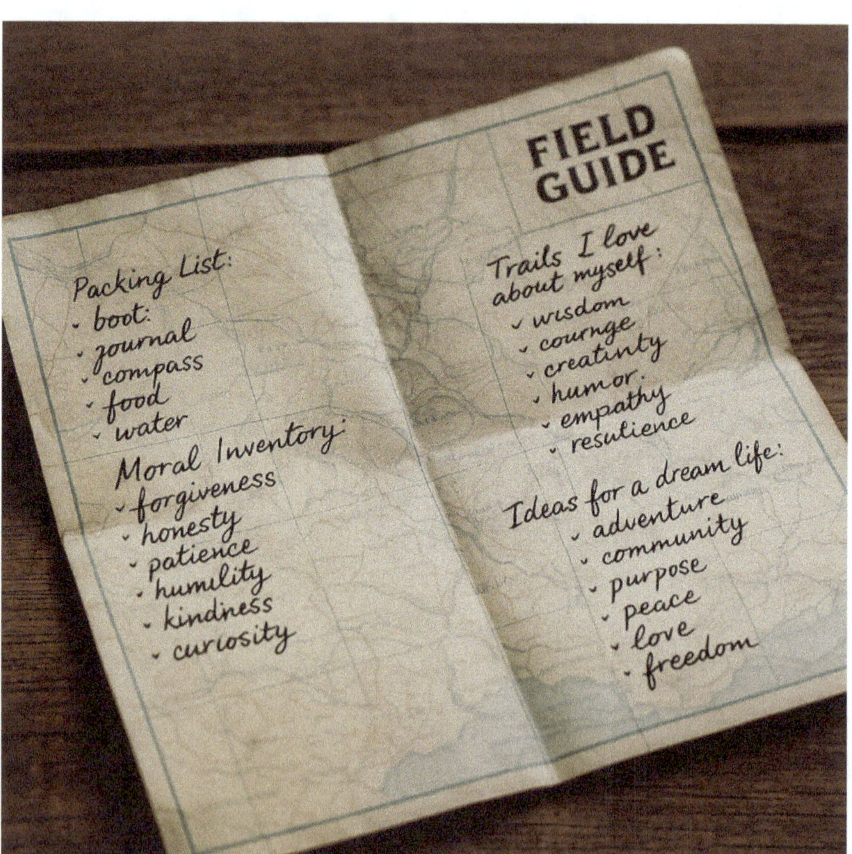

FIELD GUIDE

Packing List:
- boot:
- journal
- compass
- food
- water

Moral Inventory:
- forgiveness
- honesty
- patience
- humility
- kindness
- curiosity

Trails I love about myself:
- wisdom
- courage
- creativity
- humor.
- empathy
- resilience

Ideas for a dream life:
- adventure
- community
- purpose
- peace
- love
- freedom

LISTS – GOTTA LOVE THEM!

LIFE IS CRAZY! LISTS KEEP ME FROM SETTING SHIT ON FIRE.

Wondering What Qualifies as a List?

There's more to lists than meets the eye—more than most humans give them credit for, more than most people even begin to believe or fathom. There are *to-do lists*, single-file checklists for groceries or garden chores. There are *should/shame lists* and *pissed-off pissy lists* of what makes me mad. There are *people lists* for invitations, boundaries, or birthdays. Calendars, once plans and events are added? Basically just sneaky vertical lists.

A list is just a linear, visual way to un-fog the mental windshield. It doesn't have to be pretty or color-coded or scribbled in a special planner with washi tape. It's just words in a row—tamed chaos. And it counts.

———

Don't Know Where to Start?

Grab a pen. Open Notes. Use your phone, the back of a receipt, your arm—whatever. Just get it *out*. Write down everything you need to do today. Or everyone you need to forgive. Or all the things that are bugging you. Or the steps between where you are and the dream you don't quite believe you're allowed to have yet.

You don't have to organize it. You don't even have to read it twice. The magic starts when it leaves your brain and hits the page.

And if you've got a decision to make—one that's chewing through your sleep and circling like a hawk over your gut—then try what Ben Franklin did. No, really.

———

Why Bother with Lists Anyway?

- **They unclog the swirl.** Your brain isn't a storage unit. It's a processor. When you dump your mental clutter onto a page, you're not being dramatic—you're making space for actual clarity.

- **Counting Blessings vs. Burdens:** A popular example would be a Gratitude List, the idea is simple: write down everything you're grateful for that comes to mind: "I can hear. I have coffee. A cat that tolerates me. I don't have cancer." It's not about being profound—it's about noticing what's not currently a dumpster fire. Even a quick list can shift your lens, reroute your mood, and remind you that not *everything* sucks.

- **They make things visible.** Sometimes the loop sounds like: "I have so much to do, I'm so behind, I'll never catch up." A list says: "Actually, it's six things. One of them is flossing."

- **They're forgiving.** Cross it out. Rewrite it. Toss it. Circle the same damn thing every day until you're ready to do it. Lists don't care. They don't shame. They wait.

- **They change how decisions feel.** Something about seeing your options written down—without the swirling panic of feeling it all at once—lets your body exhale. It's the opposite of a mental pressure cooker. Once I go through the process, I almost always feel *more confident* in my decision. The clarity becomes visceral.

- **They open the channel.** Once the swirl quiets, your DMGS can actually get a word in. Lists clear the static. Insight gets airtime. Guidance lands. Sometimes the answer is already in the list—you just had to see it.

- **Ben Franklin did it.** In a 1772 letter to Joseph Priestley, he wrote: *"To get over this, my Way is, to divide half a Sheet of Paper by a Line into two Columns, writing over the one Pro, and over the other Con… Then during three or four Days Consideration I put down… short Hints… When I have… estimated their respective Weights… and… strike them both out…*

———

Field Guide Moment: Do Your Own Benny List

Got a decision spinning in your brain? Stop looping and grab a piece of paper. Draw a line down the middle: label one side **Pro**, the other **Con**.

Over the next few days, jot things down as they come to you. Don't overthink it. Just notice.

Then start crossing off anything that carries the same weight on both sides. One for one. Keep going until what's left is clear—or at least clearer than it was.

No overanalyzing. No spreadsheet required. Just a quiet little nudge toward your own knowing.

———

FIELD GUIDE RULE #10: WHEN IN DOUBT, LIST IT OUT.

FREEDOM
ACCEPTANCE
ACCEPTANCE
TRUST

MEDITATION: THOUGHTS REQUIRED

DON'T JUST DO SOMETHING - SIT THERE!

Wondering about "meditation?"

It's not what you think. Seriously. Forget the stereotypes. You don't have to chant, sit like a pretzel, "cancel" every thought, or become the Dalai Lama overnight. For me, when I first tried it years ago, it meant sitting still without distractions. Which sounded… fucking painful. And it was. So painful, I couldn't do it for long. My brain was loud, my body was twitchy, and everything felt like an excuse to quit. I was uncomfortable—not calm—and I could not stop yawning for the life of me.

Now, meditation is my access to the invisible shit that's running me. It's the free and wildly underrated way I shift from being the hands-up, screaming, first-car passenger on the roller coaster of life to watching the whole ride from a comfy theater seat with popcorn. Same drama, but now I'm just noticing… "Oh hey, there's that old fear again. Look at her go!"

There are also days when the body or mind rebels—too twitchy, too wired, too wild—and I play *Let's Make a Deal*: focused breathing for five minutes instead of twenty. Still sweet. Still sacred. Still me, honoring the moment and keeping my word.

It informs me, reminds me, and reveals all sorts of perfectly perfect ideas, patterns, practices, people, places, things… whatever I happen to be ready to receive is right there. Or not. Sometimes it's totally quiet and calm and peaceful—and still perfectly making space for something to process or reveal itself later. The Landmark Forum folks used to call it "seeing what you didn't know you didn't know."

———

Why Bother with Meditation?

• **It reveals what's running the show.** Fear, control, old habits, body stories—you don't have to dig. Just sit still, and the loudest parts will show up uninvited.

• **It's the opposite of numbing.** Instead of zoning out, you're tuning in. Not always fun, rarely graceful, but way more honest than another scroll, snack, or self-fixation loop. Hang in there and keep zooming out… you're just the witness.

• **It gives your body and DMGS a microphone.** Your body already knows. Your guidance system already speaks. Meditation is where they finally get a word in.

• **It builds the pause.** Not just in your day—but in your thoughts, reactions, cravings, and self-talk. That moment of space changes *everything.*

• **It's unpredictable and perfectly timed.** Sometimes you'll get insight. Sometimes just yawns. Either way, something's shifting—even when it feels like nothing's happening.

———

Don't know where to start?

You need three things: a cell phone, earbuds (with or without the wire—noise canceling is nice), and a meditation app. That's it. I'm exceedingly practical here—no joke. Go shop. Get it done. You don't need an altar, a meditation cushion, or a velvet eye pillow. (Although I do recommend a blackout sleep mask if you've got one. Feels very "treat yourself.")

Download ***Insight Timer.*** There's a free version, but yes—they'll ask for your credit card and make you answer a bunch of earnest personal-growth questions. They mean well. Skip what you want. I don't care if you set an intention or record what you're grateful for or download the widget. From the home screen, just click the magnifying glass icon labeled **Library** at the bottom and search for any track by ***davidji, Mooji,*** *or* ***Sarah Blondin*** to start. Or just search for a word—trust, grief, surrender—and hit play on whatever jumps out. Don't like the voice? The background music?

The vibe? Stop, discard, and try another. There are literally hundreds of thousands of options in there. No pressure, just experiment. You'll know it when you hear it.

And yes, I'm a certified meditation teacher (for real). And I still fuss with using the app and all its functions... the Timer is cool too, once you don't need words any longer. Honestly, I should teach a class someday—not on how to meditate, but on how to use the damn app with ease and grace.

Once you've got the basics down, commit to two minutes a day. Just two. Pick a time. Pick a spot. Push play. That's it. You can always do more, but don't make it a whole thing. Keep it doable. (Google SMART goals).

And if you're like me? You'll need an accountability partner. It's amazing how helpful it is to say out loud—and promise to another human—what your specific goal and intention is: *I will listen to a meditation for two minutes a day for 30 days, and I'll text you a checkmark each day when I'm done.* Accountability partners are the bomb. But more on that in another chapter in this section... look for it if you're curious... **BUT FIRST...**

Get the practical shit in place. Then please, I beg you: *PLAY.* Do *not* be too serial (read: serious). The meditations range from one minute to an hour. Listen. Smile. Wander. This is time for you and your DMGS to settle in and start whispering.

You're not doing it wrong. You're just getting started.

Field Guide Moment: Start Small, Stay Honest

- Download Insight Timer
- Search for davidji or Sarah Blondin.
- Pick one track.
- Before you begin say this out loud (even if you feel silly):
  "I'm not fixing myself. I'm just noticing what feels good."

- Hit play.
- Listen

Bonus: Do this for two minutes a day for 30 days. Text your accountability partner a ✅ each day.

———

FIELD GUIDE RULE #12: SILENCE ISN'T EMPTY. IT'S FULL OF ANSWERS.

FIELD GUIDE RULE #14: INSIGHT REQUIRES AIRTIME.

TRUTH
RELEASE
CLARITY
NEXT STEP
FIELD JOURNAL

PEN & PAPER (OR A PENCIL, WHATEVER!)

THE MIRROR, THE TEACHER, THE OUTLET, THE FRIEND

Wondering why everyone keeps telling you to "journal" like it's a magic cure-all?

It's not magic. But it is honest. A pen and paper (or notes app, or voice memo, or scribbled napkin) can become a lifeline. Not because you're writing anything profound—but because you're letting something *out*. A thought, a feeling, a lie you've believed too long. It doesn't have to make sense. It just needs somewhere to go.

Don't Know Where to Start?

Start with what you've got: rage, confusion, joy, boredom, longing. Or just write: "I don't know what to write" until something bubbles up. Some days it's poetry, other days it's petty complaints or grief guts. All of it is welcome. I've journaled through family fights, heartbreaks, foggy brain spirals, and spiritual firestorms. My notebooks have been the silent witnesses to my most sacred moments and my messiest mistakes.

It's a place to burst, break, wonder, remember, grieve, or daydream without needing to explain. No grammar checks. No plot arcs. Just you and your soul on the page, working things out together. A paper mirror. A pressure valve. A time traveler. A trusted friend. As my poem says: *the mirror of my soul and patient teacher.*

Why Bother With Journalling Anyway?

- **Because your mind gets crowded.** Dumping thoughts onto the page can be the reset button your nervous system didn't know it needed.
- **Because clarity comes through movement.** The pen glides, the fog lifts. Sometimes. Or it doesn't—but at least the storm is now outside of you.
- **Because memory is a slippery thing.** Journals capture truth in the moment—even the ugly stuff— before your brain tries to rewrite it.
- **Because peace is portable.** A journal can go with you anywhere. No appointment necessary. Just open and unload.
- **Because being heard, even by yourself, heals.** You don't need a reply. Just a release.
- **Because Morning Pages are a thing.** Julia Cameron's practice from ***The Artist's Way***—two longhand pages of unfiltered writing every morning—is equal parts brain drain, creative catalyst, and truth serum. Try it for a week. You might just meet yourself on page two.

———

Try This Field Guide Moment:

Practical advice? Buy a spiral notebook or journal—yes, go shopping, you have my permission. Make it pretty or cool or especially cool. You don't need one with prompts, quotes, or bible verses (unless that lights you up). Just my opinion: skip the pre-processed stuff. Oh—and get one pen you love. Watch out, I'm a total pen hoarder. You only *need* one… but two works. Or three. ;-)

Get out of bed. Pee. Make coffee or tea. And yeah, you'll probably need to get up ten minutes earlier if you've got peeps depending on you for the morning circus. Then crack open that new, must-have journal and write. Big if you want—takes up more space on the page (smirk smirk). Two full pages. Just do it. No one will ever read it. Not even you. Unless you want to.

Start with:

"Right now, I'm feeling…"

or

"This is probably dumb, but…"

and see what lands.

Bonus: Mash up two tools: *Accountability Partners* and *Pen & Paper.* Make a weeklong commitment—two pages a day. Text your buddy that you did it. (The check-in, not the writing. NO ONE will see the actual pages unless you decide to share. Ever.)

P.S. A love note to my own journalling, penned 1989!

Pen & Paper

You are my outlet,
Where I burst emotions
Explode on paper.

How long now have you been
my friends, confidants,
peacemakers

How many sleepless nights,
gray dawns, fire lit evenings,
and summer sunsets
you have been with me.

Soaking up my dreams and fears?
Reflecting deep hurt,
Lonesome tears?
Straightening twisted thoughts?
Turning angry, wicked feelings
Into lessons learned?

Yielding always,

In the end,
At least relief,
If not true peace.

Yes, you are my friends,
Through family quarrels,
Puppy love and broken hearts,
Wounded spirit and grand achievement -
But mostly melancholy days.

Through life
In life
With life,
My life
You are my friends
The mirror of my soul
And patient teacher.

Laurie Anne Hogue (my maiden name), 1989

SHRINKS, GURUS, MENTORS & CRONES

THEY MIGHT HELP. JUST DON'T LET THEM HIJACK YOUR GLOW

Wondering who counts as a "helper"?

We're talking sponsors, therapists, mentors, acupuncturists, coaches, nutritionists, spiritual teachers, wise aunts, semi-feral fairy godmothers, or the lady who reads your aura at the farmer's market. They come in all forms. Some are paid. Some are cosmic gifts. Most are flawed, just like you.

Don't Know Where to Start?

Start by getting clear. Ask yourself: What do I *think* I need? Advice? A listening ear? A plan? A pattern interrupt? Get specific—even if it's messy. Then—dial a friend, ask for a referral, be picky, read reviews, be thorough (without overthinking—*aka fear and control*). Interview a couple of potentials. Pay attention to your gut. Ask questions. Be honest. Don't let unspoken expectations rule the relationship (they can't read your mind). If something feels weird or off —*walk*. You're allowed to change your mind. Always.

And also—watch for the weird. Sometimes the total opposite of "getting clear" is the real invitation. Like when a workshop on mantras or releasing trapped emotions shows up just as you're craving emotional freedom or a deeper meditation practice. Coincidence? Maybe. Or maybe not. Either way—go ahead. Take the fucking weird-ass cosmic bait. The Universe *might* be dropping breadcrumbs toward your next breakthrough or Trail Head. Follow them—or better yet, study their map, check out their tools, compare and contrast. Accept, enjoy, or enthuse. Or thank them kindly and walk on to the next trail guide.

Why Bother with Other Humans Anyway?

Because sometimes we really do need backup. Trained professionals can help rewire long-term patterns. Sponsors can spot your sabotage from a mile away. A skilled bodyworker might help you move trauma you didn't even know was stuck. But always remember: the ultimate answer is *inside you*. There is no distance, no waiting, no admission fee for the truth you already carry. So yes—seek support. But beware of obsessive clinging, codependency, or performing to please. The best relationships empower your own knowing, not override it.

What about Retreats? Classes? Courses?

Books you can close. People you can avoid. But retreats… they wrap you in a bubble of intentionality, snacks, and spiritual playlists. Whether online or in person, they tend to come dressed in white or branded in beige—and often echo the voice of a single teacher, book, or healing modality. They can be beautiful. Or brutal. Or both. What matters is the same: Check your motive. Stay awake. If you find yourself detoxing on day three and questioning your entire life, fantastic. If you're just there for the smoothies and spiritual merch, also fine. Just don't confuse wisdom with worship or groupthink with grace.

Emotional processing tools "Out There", smudging, gibberish meditations (it's for real and lovely), cleansing rituals, Emotion Code, healing circles, Eat Right for Your Type, Personal Power, Be a Practitioner of XYZ, Reiki Master Class, Crystal Singing Bowl Sound Therapy Expert, The Fury Cleanse - I'm making these up. Sort of, anyway you get the idea. Explore them all freely, but with discernment. Some tools heal. Some distract. You'll know. But only if you ask. Ask first. Meditate on any retreat, class, or healing detour before you go. Tune in. Your DMGS will let you know what sticks and what's just spiritual BS or simply not necessary for you at this moment in time and space, no shade.

The message here is really about discernment, not doing. It's about not rushing to action, not outsourcing, and not bypassing your DMGS with the next shiny tool or personality.

There's no Field Guide Moment here… unless you want to attend a class I might offer someday—then all bets (and discernment) are off. *Just kidding. Sort of.*

FIELD GUIDE RULE #19: ASK FIRST. THE DMGS DOESN'T SHOUT—IT RESPONDS.

PART EIGHT
ENCORE ANYONE?
APPLAUSE, APPLAUSE...
A FEW MORE FOR THE ROAD!

You know that feeling when the lights dim, the band walks offstage, and you're not *quite* ready for it to be over? Sometimes, your favorite song is the one that comes *after* the setlist ends. These pieces feel like that—unexpected, resonant, and lingering a little longer. Had enough resonating and vibrating? Or are you up for just a bit more?

You are beautiful
You are beautiful
You are doing a great job
You are doing a great job.
I Love You!
I Love You!
SAY IT...
OUT LOUD...
(LIKE YOU FUCKING
MEAN IT)
Deal with it!
Y. McCauley 5-15-20

YOU ARE NEVER ALONE

WHEN IN DOUBT: GRAB. PULL. LISTEN. REPEAT.

The meditation experience yesterday has been more challenging than usual to articulate—like trying to catch a whisper in the wind. There was no image or word that came immediately to mind. The sensations started a couple of weeks ago during the BYOB course. At that point, the words I heard were, "I'll teach you to love." It was almost too extravagant to believe—that I could access love, much less that some internal part of me was ready to be my teacher. It felt overwhelming, like a door opening, and I didn't even attempt to put it into words. Now, though, the theme is repeating, and the sensations are becoming more believable and trustworthy... if that makes any sense.

I realize I've built such an amazing protective system—my own emotional Fort Knox—that I barely knew it was there. My behaviors were and are so ingrained that only now am I learning to decipher what is kind and what is, well, not so much. On some level, admitting this feels vulnerable, maybe even a tad embarrassing. I know that "love," like "God," triggers my defenses. I've sidestepped both words, trading them in for something more palatable, less fraught. I wrote them off as too generic, overused, or packed with associations I wasn't ready to unpack. They came loaded with guilt and sadness, worthiness and lack. The other day, I was watching movie trailers and realized just how much Hollywood has tried to define love for us—sunsets, slow-motion kisses, tragic misunderstandings. They make you feel as though they've cornered the market on defining love. But expectations are a funny thing; they lead to judgment, comparison, manipulation, and control. And, of course, once those enter the picture, love (and God) quietly slips out the back door.

Looking back, I'm amazed and astounded at how far I've come.

I didn't set out to redefine love with this journey. My goal was to bring my soul and personality into alignment, to quiet the nasty inner critic that's made a home in my head. Along the way, it felt right to become a friend to my body, to actually try befriending my physical self. It's funny, but that's something I hadn't tried before. I've negotiated with my "inner rebel" at times, even made some headway, but befriending myself? That was new territory.

And here I am now, with this unexpected invitation—an opening I hadn't anticipated. I'm only 29 days into this practice, and I'm looking forward to seeing where this journey of self-compassion leads. Befriending my body is like learning a new language—awkward at first, but with a little practice, surprisingly rewarding. It's little things, like listening to what I need or taking a few minutes to just breathe. And I'm grateful for the mantras I've adopted lately. Simple words, maybe, but they feel like shelter and direction when I need them most: There is nothing to fear. There is nothing to prove. There is nothing to fix. There is nothing wrong, and there is nothing missing.

Each mantra brings its own kind of sanity. "Nothing to fear" invites courage, a reminder that life is safe to explore and that fear is 90% delusional. "Nothing to prove" tells me to let go of perfectionism, to stop comparing and judging my worth based on others' expectations I've unknowingly taken on. "Nothing to fix" is a potent reminder that, most likely, "it's not my circus and not my monkeys." The chances are high that I am not responsible for fixing anything because, with a slight shift in perspective, everything is perfectly perfect as it is. And "nothing is missing" is my favorite of all—a deep reassurance that everything I need is already here within me.

Each phrase whispers a different invitation: release worry, drop expectations, step back from control, recognize completeness. These words are like a gentle hand on my shoulder, guiding me away from the need to do and toward the ability to simply be. With each reminder, I feel a bit closer to the friend I want to be to myself, someone who offers gentleness instead of judgment, who listens rather than insists.

So, here's to 29 more days of not tripping over my own self-discovery—and a big shout-out to my Guardian for the patience of a saint. Many thanks to whomever is tuning in to assist with this transmission. All is well.

COFFEE, CONTROL AND THE COUNCIL WITHIN

MEDITATION, MOVEMENT, AND MUTUAL RESPECT REQUIRED

Friendship is one thing, but partnership? That's a whole new level. This journey of self-discovery has surprised me with insights I didn't even know I needed—like the realization that my relationship with my body isn't just about making nice and being friendly. It's about collaboration, teamwork, and even a little trial and error.

When I started this journey, I believed I had no self-love and zero idea how to take care of my body. I saw myself as judgmental and mean, a negligent caretaker at best. My efforts were emergency-only responses—foxhole prayers to get me through a crisis. Sure, I'd hit up a detox spa or squeeze in an annual physical, but mostly, I manipulated my body with food, alcohol, nicotine, and the occasional massage or acupuncture session. I assumed my track record was awful.

But surprise! Turns out I wasn't as terrible as I thought. According to my inner voice, I've done an excellent job navigating the trials and tribulations of being in a human body. Who knew? Sure, I was judgmental and mean at times—no delusion there—but I wasn't the hopeless case I imagined.

Initially, my goal was simple: to befriend my body. I figured friendship would mean showing up consistently and listening. That's about as far as I'd gotten. But now, the door is open, trust is blossoming, and the experience with coffee is proof. Slowly, I'm learning to step back from dictator mode and let my body have a say.

And then came the curveball: this isn't just about friendship—it's a partnership. The words in this piece of art came floating by clear as a bell in my meditation a couple of days ago. We, the body, mind, spirit and emotions are not just friends, we're partners!

This is my jam! Partnership feels professional, organized. It's about cooperation, collaboration, and clear communication. The images that came to me during meditation were all about teamwork—a team where my body, mind, and soul are all active players. For whatever odd reason, I feel more at home in a partnership than a friendship. It feels solid and dependable, like something I can count on. Each part brings something unique to the table. The body shows up with its signals and needs, the mind processes and plans, the spirit offers perspective, and emotions give everything a little color. Together, we're figuring it out, one step at a time.

But let's be real: the partnership is a work in progress. I keep noticing tidbits of resistance and attachment—polarities that create discord. My attachment to being thin fuels my resistance to accepting how I look now. These two forces are locked in a battle that keeps me spinning my wheels. If I wasn't searching for a long term unique solution through meditation, I'd probably be on another yo-yo diet and cycling through detailed exercise plans that I'd abandon after a few days.

And then there's coffee—my old pal. Coffee used to be my ride-or-die buddy. But now? It's that friend who overstays their welcome, leaving you with a sour stomach and the realization that maybe you've outgrown them. The fact that I've been quietly weaning myself off without any grand declarations or rebellious backlash? Honestly, that feels like a miracle.

So what does partnership look like in practice? For starters, it means listening. When I'm stuck in judgmental, comparing, self-hating thoughts, I'm learning to collaborate with my feelings—both mentally and physically. Like today, when I was spiraling, I did a quick five-minute indoor walk. That tiny shift got me out of my head and back into my body.

And that's what partnership looks like—collaborating with your feelings and your body, moving through the hard stuff one step (or quick indoor walk) at a time. It's not perfect, and it doesn't have to be. But this too shall pass. And when it does, I'll still be here, showing up for the team.

This one floated in like a wink from the universe—equal parts ancient knowing and playful reminder. I didn't sit down to write a poem, I sat down to remember something I'd almost forgotten. Life isn't a punishment or a puzzle to solve. It's a game. A treasure hunt. A deeply personal, often hilarious, sometimes maddening adventure in trust and love and letting go.

And once you stop trying to win or finish or get it right—once you let the heart speak—you start to hear it whisper: "Love the gamc." Enjoy.

Love the Game
I feel it rising--
a spark, a pull,
a plan not of the mind
but of the heart.
A wish.
A dream.
A soul-deep signal
I can almost remember.

My soul has a hunch.
A scent on the wind,
a shimmer on the path.
This is not new.
It's a treasure hunt--
Hide & seek
across lifetimes...

A game I've played
for centuries.
And centuries more
will unfold before it's done.

Enjoy THIS journey.

Stop asking why.
Just **play the game**,
Be bliss, now.
All is well--
so says my heart to me.

Beyond what eyes can see,
trust is alive.
Each moment brims--
no waiting, no holding back.
Just dive in.
No worries.

The bonds I form,
the skills I gather--
they'll travel with me
into the next round.
So Love, scoop them up--
both the pain and the pleasure,
the agony, the awe.
No harm, no foul.

You're collecting treasures.
Each one,
a different face
of the same sacred coin.
Perhaps or not.
No matter.

So trust the game.
Play full out.
And when in doubt—laugh.
A lot.

Because really--

there's no prize for suffering,
no points for perfection,
no villain,
no flaw,
no missing piece.

And I am certain, truly—
there's nothing to fear,
nothing to fix,
nothing to prove,
nothing wrong,
and absolutely nothing missing.

Tag, you're it.
Game on.

- March 2025

BE

FEARLESSLY

KIND

unconditionally

4·26·20

TIA

GOING TO ANY LENGTHS

WHICH LENGTH?
WHERE? HOW'S THAT?

Going to any lengths—what does that even mean anymore? I signed back into FitnessPal the other day and guess what? I still had a login from *2014*. Are you fucking kidding me? That's eight years ago. EIGHT. And here I am, still spinning the same damn wheel about weight and fitness goals. Zero progress? Well… not exactly. I mean, I did stop drinking in 2014. I quit smoking the year after. I (mostly) kicked sugar's ass in 2020. I waded through the hormonal jungle of menopause—past tense, hopefully. I retired. I moved into my dream home, my forever space with more freedom and nature than I could've dreamed of. All of that is real. That's not nothing. That's actual, tangible growth. And yet—here I sit, still out of shape, still overweight, still thinking about it. Every. Damn. Day.

This time, though, I asked a new question: *How can I actually approach this differently?* Not with the same recycled willpower and white-knuckled plans. But truly different. Not "lose 20 pounds before X" or "track every damn bite," but something with an ounce of sanity. Like… what if I just moved consistently? Not out of punishment, but joy. What if I created a simple, sustainable, mostly enjoyable routine that got me outside, or sweaty, or both—but didn't feel like torture? And what if, instead of obsessing over macros and meal timing, I simply ate healthy, satisfying food when I was actually hungry? That's it. That's the goal. Two goals, actually: *Move often. Eat like I love myself.* I can almost hear my inner self blinking back tears, whispering: "Finally."

Of course, I've tried it all before. Noom, Weight Watchers, Eat Right for Your Type, the Crazy Sexy Diet, plant-based everything, belly busting plans, alkaline resets, Diets Don't Work (ironically), Intuitive Eating, the whole damn alphabet soup. And now I'm back full circle to FitnessPal. Trial, error, trial, error, repeat. I won't call it failure—because I *have* learned. But damn if I'm not exhausted. I'm ready to be done. To be neutral. To be… unhooked from the conversation entirely. I love food. I love cooking. I want to love movement, too. I want my energy back. Maybe this is a new bottom. Or maybe it's the one I've hit enough times to finally get up from—for good.

So why am I here, writing this, planning to actually post it? Because this year—2022—my word was *UNITY.* Not *alignment,* which I prayed for for years. (Did I just say pray? Stop the presses. That's a story for another day.) Alignment, it turns out, is more like a strategic alliance of parts. But unity… unity is different. It's a complete, harmonious whole. A coming-together. That word dropped in like a whispered command, and suddenly I saw how long I'd been at war with myself—fragments trying to cooperate, rather than unify. That tiny shift in language cracked something open.

That crack led me here. Signing up for a Hay House 4-day free writing challenge—on a whim. Showing up. Writing about this *godforsaken, never-ending, always-evolving* health/fitness saga. Not to fix it. Not to solve it. But to *see it.* To name it. To sit with it in words instead of shame. To find even a flicker of compassion in the mess. And wouldn't you know it, *writing* about it has been the most healing thing I've done in a long time. It reminds me of what **David Sedaris said in his MasterClass**—that some people go through hell and don't write about it. He couldn't imagine surviving anything awful without turning it into a story. (That's a terrible paraphrase, sorry David. Take his class. It's brilliant.) I get it now. Writing is my release valve. My alchemy. My sanity.

So what does going to any lengths actually mean? I thought it meant counting every calorie, walking ten thousand steps, sticking to the plan. But maybe it means *telling the truth.* Staring into the mirror without flinching. Choosing unity over the illusion of control. Writing it out instead of stuffing it down. Today, that's enough. Maybe tomorrow, too. I'm still here. Still believing in magic. And snacks. Always snacks.

Living
When what is
Possible
Lives
With you
And touches
All you do
Inspires
What you say
And what you
Hear transforms
Into yet another
Possibility
Unreasonable
Yet possible
Not in here
- Out there
And you send
Ripples
Far and wide
No need to hide
Fear becomes
Courage
Confrontation
Transformation
Breakdown
Breakthrough
And paradox
Lives in harmony
With all that
Is – out there
And inside

You are living.

- 2002

Trust yourself. You can do this!

TO BE A DREAM

MIC DROP!

I've been doing energy work—releasing trapped emotions that Dr. Hawkins, Dr. Nelson, and so many others have identified as the root of both physical and spiritual illness. I am profoundly grateful to have found this reliable, transformative link—the space where the obstacles to alignment with my inner truth become malleable, available for release. This morning, something shifted. Something old, something familiar yet distant.

Release
In the still, silent, calm.
Deep in the layers.
As I sift and dive,
Fly and float.
In the currents
Between the skins
And masks,
Facades and fantasies.
I sense a never-ending sorrow.
As it shifts then fades—evasive.
Below the trauma,
Before the bruises,
Ahead of birth—my birth,
Since before my beginning.

Here,
I am missing a friend.
A dream I wrote of
As a child then forgot.

Decades later, I recall.
My soul aches.

It hurts and cries,
Whimpers and wanes,
Still yearning for love
From the outside in.
A twin? A friend? A soul mate?
That someone
Who completes me,
Who allows this life
To be joyful and fulfilling.

I have been looking, searching.
Lost for so long,
At some level needy, alone,
And frightened.
Powering through,
Adapting—coping.
Waiting—hoping.
Watching—grieving.
All this time.
All these decades.
The fog is cleared.
Now I can let her go.

- January 2025

This reminded me of a poem I wrote when I was young. Back then, I'm certain I was writing about romantic love—the ideal of a perfect partner. But now, I see the truth: it was never just about a person. It was about every relationship ideal I've ever held, including the one with myself. The longing, the ache of incompleteness—it wasn't about another soul stepping in to complete me. It was my own reflection, distorted by time and longing, whispering to be found.

In doing this energy work, I've uncovered something even more important than the release of ensnared emotions: I've found the emerald thread of my soul, the part of me that has always been there, waiting to be seen. This work is not about "fixing" or "finding" something outside myself—it's about clearing away what isn't mine. The stories, the fears, the illusions that kept me searching instead of being. Now I see—what I longed for wasn't another person. It was alignment, clarity, freedom. The love I was searching for was always my own.

This journey—of healing, of release, of uncovering what was buried—has not been about gaining something new, but about reclaiming something old. The dream was never lost, only hidden beneath the weight of unspoken grief and unanswered longing. As I reread my poem from 1982, I see the echoes of my younger self in these words. I see the part of me that longed for a love that would rescue, complete, or define me. But I also see something deeper—a part of me that already knew the truth I am just now embracing. The dream is not another person. The dream is me.

To Be A Dream

If only we could see beyond today.
Seek each other out, knowing the way.
What to come accepting
With no prejudice or decepting
Knowing the legends sleeping
Deep within each other's dreaming
Seeing with eyes, not regretting
Casting through mist and netting
Seeking out what is worth remembering.

To aid the other in conquering
What hinders happiness o're taking
Sensing the one they wish to be
Actions departed, forgiving
Praying always to be "we"
And not just "he" or "she"
Working, striving, undertaking
To be a dream and help a dream to be.

Can this imagined and once realized
Break away the thin disguise
That echoes through your soul, not true
And changes once green eyes to blue
Will you help me? Can you see
The soul I truly hope to be?
Searching now through gauze
Through fog and misty trees
And be a dream and help a dream to be?

-

Present day… and so I let go—not of the dream, but of the illusion that it was ever separate from me. I trust that I am whole. I trust that I am enough. I trust that the dream is not something to be found, but something to be lived. Trust is the bridge between longing and fulfillment, between fear and freedom. It is what allows me to release the past and walk forward without hesitation, without doubt—only with openness and grace. I trust the emerald thread will always guide me home.

AFTERWORD

If you've made it all the way to this afterword, first of all—thank you. Truly. It means something to me that you wandered through these pages, paused where something resonated, skipped what didn't, and maybe even felt moved to share a moment or a line with someone you care about. That's all this Field Guide ever hoped to offer: a place to be human, in all the ways we are.

Writing this book turned into its own unexpected adventure—equal parts hilarious, humbling, surprising, and *holy crap, I did not see that coming*. I learned more by telling these stories than I ever did by studying any official method or shiny wisdom tradition. Somewhere between the wandering and the writing, something steady and kind made itself known: my DMGS is real. Not as a concept or a metaphor, but as an actual presence with its own quiet personality—patient, compassionate, and surprisingly good at orchestrating synchronicities when I'm not busy getting in the way.

If you forget everything else from this book, try remembering this: **pause**. Just pause. When things feel tangled or tense, when you're irritable, restless, or discontent—smile, if you can, and pause. Become a witness for a second. You don't have to fix or solve or analyze anything. Just notice. That tiny moment of awareness? It might be a doorway disguised as a breath.

As you close this book, I hope you carry whatever made you exhale, smirk, or feel a little lighter. Let your own inner compass speak up when it wants to. Let freedom rise from the inside, one pause at a time.

Wander well.

Stay curious.

Please remember to be gentle with yourself—you're doing better than you think.

And so, I'll close with the same poem that opened this guide, because some truths don't need embellishment - just a moment of listening. One last pause, before you go.

No Other Love

All there is to do – is listen
to your own heart
Follow your own song
to the beat of the drum within.
Do not despair or grow impatient
Like the tides ebb and flow –
as the seasons go
So turn the circles of your time.
Within each breath be grateful
Talk to me – Listen – Breathe
Gracefully your life unfolds
in time's time with wisdom and magic.
There is no other time but now.
There is no other love but ours.

- January 2019

ABOUT THE AUTHOR

Laurie Anne McCauley is a space creator, lifelong journaler, and curious wanderer of both inner and outer landscapes. After a thirty-year corporate career working across all fifty states—supporting K–12 school food and nutrition programs as a software program designer, project manager, technical writer, trainer, and translator of complex systems into plain, usable language for the fantastic women who feed our children every day—she eventually turned her attention to the quieter terrain within.

Throughout her career, Laurie created R&D documentation, user training manuals, and quick reference guides (QRGs) designed to make real life doable—sometimes on a single sheet of paper, front and back. Long before she named it, she had a gift for breaking down complicated ideas, stripping away unnecessary noise, and leaving behind what actually helps. Apparently, she's been writing field guides her whole life.

A natural organizer and lifelong learner, Laurie has always been interested in how people change from the inside out: what supports clarity, what gets in the way, and what happens when we pause long enough to listen. She doesn't claim to have answers for anyone else. She writes to map her own lived experience and to offer companionship along the way, blending insight, humor, vulnerability, and a dash of sass.

Born in Boulder, Colorado, Laurie now lives near Saratoga Springs, New York, with her partner and a rotating cast of beloved furry friends. There, she continues to write, adventure, meditate, tend plants, sing, create space, and follow a not-so-linear path toward greater ease, clarity, and joy—one honest moment at a time.